THERE IS MORE TO MILK AND HONEY

Louis Palmisano

ISBN 979-8-89130-821-3 (paperback)
ISBN 979-8-89243-128-6 (hardcover)
ISBN 979-8-89130-822-0 (digital)

Copyright © 2024 by Louis Palmisano

All rights reserved. No part of this publication may be reproduced, distributed, or transmitted in any form or by any means, including photocopying, recording, or other electronic or mechanical methods without the prior written permission of the publisher. For permission requests, solicit the publisher via the address below.

Christian Faith Publishing
832 Park Avenue
Meadville, PA 16335
www.christianfaithpublishing.com

Printed in the United States of America

Preface

The reason I named the book *There Is More To Milk and Honey* was that a coworker of mine was leaving the dealership, and he told me that he was going to California, the land of milk and honey. In my mind, I thought that was how the name of milk and honey originated; how could I have been so naive?

My first poem, "Milk and Honey," told how I got the revelation and how it had impacted my life. From that day on, my life was never the same. I thank God every day for leading me to Him.

Inside Information about the Author

This book is a collection of poems written by the author. Most of them were written after he was diagnosed with stage four cancer. Some of his poems were written in the middle of the night, when he was awoken from a deep sleep. Remember this: The poems that you are about to read aren't stories. "For the things that come out of a person's mouth, come from the heart" (Matthew 15:18).

Now, What?

Toward the end of this book, there is a statement that reads, "Now, What?" What are you going to do? Put the book away, let it collect dust, and keep taking the same road, expecting it to get you somewhere else. That's how I was a few years ago. Then I picked up a Bible and started writing poems that changed my life. As you are reading this, is your spiritual life important to you? Now, what?

The Last Years of My Life

Let's go back to two thousand Nineteen,
When I was faced with reality, not just a bad Dream.
I am going to tell a story that must be Told,
It started off with the death of my mother, who died on Mother's Day,
She was one hundred years Old.
She was admitted to the hospital because her lungs were Wet,
I thought she would be out in a couple of days I would have Bet.
A couple of days have gone By,
And the doctors told me that she is going to Die.
And the very next night, she passed Away,
That is something that we all have to do Someday.
But the story doesn't end There,
I have a lot to tell you, a lot to Share.
A couple of weeks later, I noticed that my urine was a reddish Tan,
I went to the doctor, and he ordered a CT Scan.
The results were in; I was dying to Hear,
What he told me was my greatest Fear.
Stage four kidney cancer, he Said,
Then to the lungs, vena cava, and arm, it had Spread.
Then he gave me the name of another doctor to Call,
He was a surgeon at Ochsner who was on Call.
He is a specialist in this Field,
I was told that he is the real Deal.
The doctor was sent a copy of the Test,
He was going to evaluate it and do what is Best.
He called me the next day with the News,
And when he talked about the situation, it gave me the Blues.
He told me, Do not come to the appointment set for Tomorrow,

As he spoke, with his voice filled with Sorrow.
He told me that there is nothing that he can do; I will be dead in less
    than one Year,
Hearing that, my eyes started to Tear.
Now I had to go and tell my Wife,
She is in the kitchen signing up her mother for hospice, and her heart
    is filled with Strife.
I saw the hurt in her Eyes,
The kind of hurt when someone Dies.
The next couple of days were hard to Take,
My mind was reeling; my life was at Stake.
I called MD Anderson Hospital and made an appointment There,
I met an oncologist, a doctor of compassion, a doctor of Care.
She looked at me with hope in her Eyes,
She gave me the will to fight, the will to Survive.
She said that we are going to try an immune therapy called Keytruda,
Which is New,
And she also told me that the side effects are Few.
I left her office that Day,
With a feeling of hope that no one can take Away.
I took the medicine prescribed for two months, every Day,
Then I had a reaction: I hate to Say.
I was unable to drink or eat anything at All,
While being admitted to St. Tammany Hospital, I could barely walk
    down the Hall.
On my very first day in the hospital, my minister Tim and his wife
    Marcia came to visit Me,
He said, "Louie, can I say a prayer?" he got down on one Knee.
My wife and Marcia also got down to Pray,
It was a very humbling experience, I have to Say.
So when he began to pray, I closed my Eyes,
And what happens next is a one-in-a-lifetime Surprise.
When I close my eyes to listen to Tim Pray,
I see the whole room in the light of the Day.
Then I grab my eyes frantically to see if they are Closed,
Then I came to my senses and tried to stay Composed.

Listen to this, as my eyes were closed TIGHT,
A vision came in SIGHT.
A black man and woman walked in and stood by the WINDOWSILL,
Not moving, just standing perfectly STILL.
He was wearing a green suit, and she had on this flowered, colored DRESS,
My head is reeling now, and my mind is a MESS.
Then I took a second LOOK,
The woman in the flowered dress is holding a big BOOK.
Could it be the book of life, which I know is TRUE?
Read Revelation 20:15, not found in the Old Testament but found in the NEW.
All of a sudden, out of the corner of this vision, something gets my ATTENTION,
It is two dark bronze men that I must MENTION.
Now remember, my eyes are still CLOSED,
And I see these two huge men sparsely CLOTHED.
They walked in and stopped by my bed, one on the left, the other on my RIGHT,
Two bare-chested muscular men, arms folded—what a SIGHT!
My heart was beating so FAST,
Watching these four people, I was wondering, *How long will this LAST?*
While my vision was fixed on these two MEN,
Tim's prayer finally came to an END.
I then opened my eyes, and all four were GONE,
The man, the woman, and the BRAWN.
I told Tim the vision that I HAD,
He looked at me and said, "You should be GLAD."
Those were angels. I said, "Are you kidding ME?"
Now I know what the Bible meant when it said, "I will never leave thee, nor forsake THEE" (Hebrews 13:5).
The Bible tells a story like nothing I have read BEFORE,
It will bring you closer to God and Jesus, whom I love and ADORE.
I am going to speed forward, if that's OKAY,
I have a lot on my mind that I must SAY.
I stayed at St. Tammany Hospital for about a WEEK,

They put a feeding tube up my nose because I couldn't EAT.
After one week went BY,
I still could not eat; they thought I was going to DIE.
So I was then transferred to Ochsner in Jefferson PARISH,
Everyone thought, including me, that I was going to PERISH.
I then spent a week at Ochsner, getting transfusion after TRANSFUSION,
But I still cannot eat; confused, I thought I was having an ILLUSION.
My friends, Tim and Ken, came to visit me one NIGHT,
I had lost a lot of weight; I was a SIGHT.
While they were there, the doctors came IN,
And spoke about what kind of shape I was IN.
The doctors said that my outlook isn't GOOD,
I wasn't responding to the medicine the way they thought I WOULD.
Tim and Ken saw that my body was fading FAST,
About this time, my wife's phone rang; it was MD Anderson on the
    LINE,
It seemed that they called just in the nick of TIME.
It seems my daughter Leslie called them on the phone and told them
    about my CONDITION,
And they called Ochsner tonight to see if they would transfer me
    with their PERMISSION.
When Tim and Ken heard this, they took the doctors OUTSIDE,
And before I knew it, I was in an ambulance at 5:00 o'clock, taking
    a RIDE.
It was a terrible ride. I have to SAY,
Riding in a medal creeper all the WAY.
It took us about six hours to get THERE,
MD Anderson Hospital is known for extreme cancer CARE.
It's the policy of MD Anderson that all transfer patients before admis-
    sion are checked out in TRAUMA,
Little did I know that the stage was set for DRAMA.
My heart rate went up from sixty beats per MINUTE,
To 220 beats a MINUTE.
They didn't know what was happening to ME,
So I told them that I have SVT.
SVT is a heart CONDITION,

4

Where speed is its Mission.
They gave me a shot in the Arm,
After a few minutes, my body and heart became Calm.
After that, they had to get a hospital room Ready,
My heart was beating slowly and Steady.
Now I am in my room, feeling kind of Weak,
And the doctors told me that they would start a transfusion, the first
    of the Week.
In order to administer this transfusion, they had to drill a hole in my
    Neck,
Believe me, I was in no position to Object.
A team of five came into my room to do the Procedure,
They started right away. I was their main Feature.
They told my wife it would be best if she wasn't There,
I understand it would have been hard for her to Bear.
As they started the procedure, I got a rush to my Head,
It's happening again. I was having an episode of SVT, right in the Bed.
They told me to calm Down,
As if I had any control, I kind of made a Frown.
They all were yelling, "Code blue! Code Blue!"
I sure hoped that they knew what to Do.
They called my wife and said, "It's an emergency, and to come back Up,"
I guess she thought that my time was Up.
I looked around, so many nurses and doctors, I counted over Thirty,
When my wife came, she wanted to call the Clergy.
Finally, my wife was by my Side,
We look at the doctors, and they look confused, trying to Decide.
One doctor had a defibrillator paddle in his Hand,
The other doctor was getting a syringe off of the Nightstand.
I said, "Doc, please no paddle. Give me the Shot,"
I have been here before. Believe me, it will work on the Spot.
When he gave me the shot, I felt my heart put on the Brakes,
I said, "Thank you, doc. You knew what it Takes."
As they finished the procedure, I thanked everyone as they walked
    out of the Door,
And my wife went and finished her shopping at the Bookstore.

5

But before the transfusion could BEGIN,
They began shocking my muscles through my SKIN.
They were trying to diagnose if I had a certain type of DISEASE,
The shock was so intense over an hour that it brought me to my
    KNEES.
I remember this day, April 14, 2021. I thought I was DONE,
The next day or so, they started a nuclear DRIP,
I saw five hanging bags on the side of my bed. I thought I was going
    to FLIP.
The nurse had to wear special CLOTHES,
Their bodies were covered completely, including the face and NOSE.
Also, while I was there, my minister Tim and his wife Marcia paid a
    little visit. That was really NEAT,
After thirty-five days without eating, they saw me EAT.
I was in the hospital about thirty-five days in ALL,
Including rehab on the first floor, down the HALL.
In those thirty-five days, my wife slept in a chair by my SIDE,
Never leaving once, not even to take a RIDE.
This all happened in November two thousand NINETEEN,
Believe me, guys, it seems like a bad DREAM.
Ever since that last day in NOVEMBER,
I have not had one drop of chemo that I can REMEMBER.
After a few months have gone by, my doctor said that she wants to
    use radio wave frequency to burn up my TUMOR,
That's right, do it with a needle; it's not just a RUMOR.
But before they fixed that SITUATION,
They wanted me to address my SVT with a heart ABLATION.
This is the one time I didn't play AROUND,
I checked in at Memorial Herman Hospital, had it fixed, and now
    my heart is SOUND.
I went back to MD Anderson, and they did the procedure with radio
    WAVES,
Now I am looking forward to a tumor-free kidney and happy DAYS.
I was put on a four-month rotation to visit my doctor and get the
    results of my CT SCAN,
The last time I was there, she upped it to a five-month SPAN.

But before I forget, I want to tell you about some dreams that I HAD,
Some made me happy, and some made me SAD.
The first dream that I had took place at Leslie's house, and I couldn't
      fall ASLEEP,
So I remembered that when I was a kid, I used to count SHEEP.
And it worked. I was out in no TIME,
But when I woke up, remembering that dream blew my MIND.
I remembered in the dream that I fell asleep on number one hundred
      and FIFTY-THREE,
Could God be talking to ME?
You see, the number of fish, 153, that was CAUGHT,
Reminded me in the Bible what I was TAUGHT.
You see, in Matthew 4:19, Jesus said, "Come follow me and I will
      make you fishes of MEN,"
Jesus first said this to two apostles, then to the remaining TEN.
All of these dreams and visions aren't just in my MIND,
They are put there by our heavenly Father, who is so DIVINE.
In another dream that I had, I was at my daughter's house again,
      spending the NIGHT,
Going to MD Anderson the next morning to get my CT scan and see
      if everything was ALL RIGHT.
In my dream, there was this bright strobe LIGHT,
It woke me up in the middle of the NIGHT.
It was a blinking strobe light that spelled the word "arista," that's
      A-R-l-S-T-A,
For me to stay asleep, there was no WAY.
It woke me up at 5:00 o'clock from a deep SLEEP,
Everyone was still sleeping. I didn't make a PEEP.
Wide awake, I looked up the meaning of arista ONLINE,
When I read the Latin meaning of it, it blew my MIND.
The Latin word for arista is harvest. Did you hear what I just SAID?
Jesus will send His angels, and they will harvest the DEAD.
Matthew 13:37–42,
But that dream does not end THERE,
There is so much more that I have to SHARE.
Remember my dream at my daughter's house the night BEFORE?

Well, today, in real life, I am going for the CT scan. You have no idea what is in Store.

Remember the word arista that I dreamt about last Night?

Well, I am going to bring our God and heavenly Father into the Light.

When I lay down and was scooted into the CT machine, looking up, the word arista was written on the ceiling Tile,

When I saw that, I just started to Smile.

Soon my emotions took over, and I had to Cry,

The nurse working the CT machine saw me crying, and she asked Why.

When I told her my story, she started to Cry,

The nurse said, "Sir, please take a picture and tell everyone your Story,"

I did that because I wanted to show all of God's Glory.

So I did, and as I was telling this story to others, I saw doubt and disbelief in their Eyes,

It hurt me to my heart because they thought that I had made this up, and it was a pack of Lies.

Now I know how an innocent man feels when he is incarcerated and put in Jail,

They think that he is lying or giving them a fairy Tale.

The next dream was about a coworker, and I dreamt that his wife was going to have a Child,

When I told him this, he spoke with a little Smile.

He said, "We have been trying for a couple of years. Now that would bring us a lot of Joy,"

A few weeks later, he told me they were going to have a baby, and it was a baby Boy.

This brings us to my last Dream,

It was about a man on my sales Team.

In this dream, I met his wife, and she began to tell me her Troubles,

And one thing that I can tell you—it wasn't all champagne and Bubbles.

She was telling me about some of her issues and Money,

It seems all of her days are dark and gloomy, not bright and Sunny.

I haven't seen or talked to her husband, I guess in about, twenty-five
   YEARS,
And here I am, dreaming about him and his wife, who is in TEARS.
When I woke up from this DREAM,
I was determined to find that salesman, who was on my TEAM.
After a few days, I was able to find his phone number; it was a CELL,
I called him on the phone, and by the tone of his voice, he wasn't
   doing that WELL.
I met him at his work and gave him a little ASSISTANCE,
And I hope and pray that I helped with his financial EXISTENCE.
It has been close to two years, and this is what I am going to SAY,
I am going to be there for him; I am not going AWAY.
It's not always about giving him money; that's not what I MEAN,
It's about being there for him and being on his TEAM.
I am going to be there in his COURT,
Because we all need help and emotional SUPPORT.
Before my dream, I did not know what his wife's first name WAS,
But God makes these dreams real; that's what he DOES.
That's right before my dream; I did not know her NAME,
But God gave it to me; he put me in the GAME.
That dream helped make my faith so STRONG,
Because now, I know that I BELONG.
We have just gone through the last four years of my LIFE,
My next earthly focus is my WIFE.
A few months ago, she was diagnosed with ALS DISEASE,
I am asking all who read—pray for her, PLEASE.
Her name is DIANE,
And like I said, we all need a helping HAND.
I am going to leave an open end to this poem and STORY,
Because God is going to show everyone His GLORY.

Milk and Honey

On Sunday, I bring my mother to church because that's what I Do,
There I was, waiting for services to start while sitting there in the Pew.
The services started and were going really Nice,
Until they came to the gospel of Christ.
He spoke about Canaan and the promised Lands,
And when I heard what he had said, I put my head in my Hands.
Because years ago, I had heard someone say that California was the land of "Milk And Honey,"
How could I have been so naive? It's not even Funny.
When he finished the gospel, he then turned the Bible toward the congregation and said, with a Nod,
And this is the word of God.
When services were over, he carried the Bible over his head and High,
I had to hold back, fighting not to Cry.
Because it just dawned on me what I have been Missing,
The word of God that I should have been Cherishing.
But all of my life, I have been told, Do not read the Bible,
Now I am thinking, *Is there someone that I can hold Liable.*
Then I looked around at the other people There,
Help them, Lord, for they don't have a Prayer (Matthew 15:13).
After all of these years, I knew that I was Done,
And I had to find a church to be my final One.
After the services, I made it home in no Time,
I went to my computer and immediately got Online,
Matthew 7:7.
I sat down in my chair. I just had to Try,
To find something about Jesus, it was do or Die.

I found eleven pages of common sayings in the Bible. It was hard to
Believe,
My mind is reeling now, and I found it hard to Conceive.
I am on fire now, and it's not going to Stop,
Four constant hours on the computer, I thought my eyes were going
to Pop.
Then I found a sight that blew me AWAY,
One hundred seventy names of Jesus still stand Today.
One hundred seventy names—did you hear what I Said?
He did all of this in three years of ministry, and then He was DEAD.
No phone, TV, or Internet to spread the Word,
Just fishermen and a tentmaker who had to be Heard.
All of this stands Today,
The body of Christ cannot be held at Bay.
From that point on, my life will never be the Same,
As for the past, I guess I have only myself to Blame.
That's all over now, and I first came to you with an open heart seek-
ing to find the Truth,
Then I came to you with a surrendered heart because I found the
Proof.
Then I had a happy heart because I rose up from Under,
Now I have a heavy heart for those who are going to Plunder.
It is now for my family and children that I Pray,
That they will seek and find the truth Someday.
For He will come like a thief in the Night,
With all of His angels and with all of His Might.
For the one thing that you don't want to hear, you See,
Are those three little words—Depart From Me.
Isn't it Funny,
I had three little words—Milk And Honey,
I am going to end this story by giving God all the Glory.

What you are about to read or hear is TRUE,

What you decide to do about it is really up to YOU.

If any of this touches your HEART (Acts 2:37),

It is God Almighty calling you to make a fresh START (1 Corinthians 7:17).

Ephesians 4:1–6, 2 Timothy 1:10, Hebrews 3:1, 1 Peter 2:9–10,

Remember, God never called you to fit IN (1 Peter 2:9).

He's calling you to turn away from SIN (Acts 3:19, Luke 5:31–32, Acts 5:31, Acts 20:21),

I know it's hard for you to come out of your comfort ZONE.

Just ask Jesus, for He died on the cross all ALONE,

That's right, you see, Jesus said, "My God, my God why have you forsaken Me" (Matthew 27:46).

These words were spoken as He was nailed, hanging on the TREE (Acts 5:30, Acts 10:39).

As you can see, I am backing up with Scripture what I SAY,

So that you can hear the truth TODAY.

The End of the Beginning

The end of the beginning—what a statement! What does it MEAN?
Is it the end of an era and the beginning of a DREAM?
Is it the end of life here on earth for ME?
And the beginning of a dream in heaven, you SEE?
This is a dream that is not found in the MIND,
But found in heaven, time after TIME.
Heaven will not happen to all of US,
Only those who do God's will and are righteous and JUST.
Remember, when you are going to meet your maker and are LOOKING,
Down the barrel of DEATH.
All pride, fear of embarrassment, or failure don't cross your BREATH
    (Psalms 56:3–4, Hebrews 13:6, Psalm 27:1, Matthew 10:28,
    Psalms 23:4, Matthew 10:28, Isaiah 41:10),
And when you come to the throne of God, you come to it BOLDLY,
But speak and guide your brother very SOULFULLY (Colossians 4:6,
    Ephesians 4:25–29, Proverbs 15:1, 1 Thessalonians 4:6–7).
Please listen to what I have to SAY,
Because tomorrow may never come, and this might be your last DAY
    (Proverbs 27:1, Matthew 6:34).
If today was the last day on earth for you to be ALIVE,
What would you do to eternally SURVIVE?
Most people spend more time planning their VACATION,
Than worrying about their eternal SALVATION.
God said, Year after year, you don't do what I SAY,
Either you don't respect me or don't believe in judgment DAY (1
    Corinthians 4:5, 2 Peter 2:4, Acts 17:31, Matthew 12:36,
    Matthew 24:36, 2 Corinthians 5:10).
We never know when He is going to come day or NIGHT,

But we do know that He will be in plain Sight (Mark 13:32, Matthew 24:36).

For when He comes, everyone will Bow,

Every man, woman, and Child (Romans 14:11, Philippians 2:10).

God promises that final judgment is coming one Day (2 Corinthians 5:10),

Just ask Moses, for he didn't listen to what God had to Say.

God told Moses to speak to the rock—that was the Plan,

He didn't listen to God, and he did not go to the promised Land (Numbers 20:7–12).

This is just one example in the Bible that shows you that you must do God's Will,

If you don't, you will be held accountable for the Bill.

The Old Testament is full of people who didn't do the will of God,

And if you read it, you will see that He did not spare the Rod.

Please go to chapter 20 in the book of Leviticus,

And see how our God is very Serious.

You see, the Old Testament is a prelude to the New Testament,

The Old Testament is the New Testament Concealed,

The New Testament is the Old Testament Revealed.

Let's go back to where we were Before,

And look at some people and see what God might have in Store.

You see, some people just go through life traveling Along,

And in their hearts, they are doing nothing Wrong.

They say I don't murder, rape, or steal. I am a good Guy,

But they don't know that they are living a Lie.

Please open up your Bible to Galatians 5:19–20 and look on that Page,

You will see sins of hatred, jealousy, envy, greed, and selfish Ambition,

And fit of Rage.

These sins were not commandments given on Mount Sinai,

But if you practice them, you will surely eternally Die.

I hate to give you this bad news, but I am here to Tell,

That if you practice those sins, you will enter the gates of Hell (Galatians 5:21).

I am not judging you; I would never do That (Matthew 7:12),

I am just telling you what's in the book, and that's a FACT.

So open up the book and give it a GLANCE,

And then you will at least have a fighting CHANCE.

Could God be saying, "I am sitting here wondering why they don't listen to ME" (Luke 11:28, James 1:19, Matthew 7:24, Malachi 2:2)?

After all, I gave up my Son, who was nailed to a TREE (John 3:16, Galatians 3:13).

I am assuming that you have a Bible to READ,

Read it. Your salvation can depend on doing that DEED.

Question: Can the Bible save SOMEONE?

You must do the will of God, says the SON (Matthew 7:21–23).

Let's look at some reasons why you don't know the TRUTH,

Maybe you didn't read the Bible, which has all of the PROOF.

Or another reason; maybe years ago you were told Don't,

Read the Bible; it's too hard to Conceive.

They would tell you, Listen to me. I will tell you what to Believe (2 Peter 2, 1 John 4:1–6, Matthew 7:15–20, 16:11–12, 2 Timothy 4:3–4, Acts 20:28–30, Jeremiah 23:16, Ezekiel 23:16),

But the Bible tells you, Do not believe any Man.

Open up the Bible and read it so that you will Understand (Hebrews 4:12, Joshua 1:8, Psalms 119:105, Revelation 1:3, Proverbs 3:1–2, Romans 15:4, 2 Timothy 2:15),

Another reason is that in the Ten Commandments, God tells you to honor your mom and Dad (Exodus 20:12).

But not to believe in false teachers who make Him really Mad (Matthew 24:24, 2 Timothy 4:3–4, Acts 20:28–30, Mark 24:24),

But maybe some grandparents didn't read the Bible as Well.

It happened so long ago; it's really too hard to Tell,

For, you see, your parents honored their parents Too.

And passed what they knew about God on to You (Colossians 2:8, Matthew 5:1–9, Mark 7:1–9, John 4:23–24, 2 Thessalonians 2:10–12),

Sadly, now they might be at Rest.

And we all know that they were doing their Best,

This has been going on for almost two thousand Years.

Believing in false teachers will bring you nothing but humbling Tears (2 Timothy 4:3–4, Matthew 7:15–17, Isaiah 8:20),

Here is where faith comes into Play.

For them, without seeing God, they cannot believe; there is no Way (Hebrews 11:1),

I get it. Without faith, many people cave into Sin.

Because they can't see God or their soul from Within,

But faith produces light when our God is out of Sight (2 Corinthians 5:7),

But God is alive, God is real, and He is here, you See.

When two or more meet in His name, like you and Me (Matthew 18:19–20),

And remember, without faith, it's impossible to please GOD (Hebrews 11:6).

Let's face it. If He is not pleased, will He spare the ROD (Proverbs 13:24),

I get it. Out of sight, out of MIND.

Not thinking about God, who is so DIVINE (Colossians 2:9),

Another reason that we do not do God's WILL.

Is that we are running wild in this world and can't stand STILL (1 John 2:15–17, Luke 9:25, James 4:4, Mark 8:36, Romans 12:21),

That's right. You have kids, work, TV, computers, alcohol, drugs, and sex all come into PLAY.

All of these things help to keep God at BAY (1 John 5:4),

That's why it's important to read the BIBLE.

If you don't, you have only yourself to hold LIABLE,

There to help us is one of the fruits of the Spirit called SELF-CONTROL (Romans 7:18, Proverbs 25:27–28, Titus 2:11–12).

Without that, our sins will continue to roll and ROLL (2 Timothy 3:1–5, 1 Timothy 3:2–3, 1 Corinthians 7:5),

Today we covered a lot of GROUND.

It's important that the doctrine be SOUND,

In Galatians 1:8–9, read that VERSE.

If any man preaches any other gospel or true doctrine of CHRIST,

He will be ACCURSED (Galatians 1:8–9).

Read it for your sake, not MINE,

It's up to you to put in the TIME.

What did God say, and what He didn't SAY?

He did say, Speak to the ROCK (Numbers 20:7),

And I will open the door when you KNOCK (Revelations 8, Colossians 4:3, Isaiah 22:22, 2 Corinthians 2:12, Matthew 7:7–8, John 10:9, John 10:7, Acts 14:27).

He didn't say that He would spare the ROD,

He did say that He is a jealous GOD (Exodus 34:14, Deuteronomy 4:24, Deuteronomy 5:9).

All the scriptures in the Bible have MEANINGS,

But they do no good if you don't do the READING.

Remember, God had a job for MAN,

To read and obey the Bible—that was His PLAN.
Believe me, it is crunch time for YOU,
You must decide what you are going to DO.
To those of you who are serious about THIS,
And are looking for a life of eternal BLISS.
I am going to give you the key to HEAVEN,
And it's not rolling the dice, hoping for a seven or ELEVEN.
These verses that I have written DOWN,
Open the book so they can be FOUND.
I beg of you. Open the Bible and LOOK,
It is right there in the BOOK.
Number 1, you must hear the Word (Romans 10:17),
Don't worry about the world. They may think that you are a NERD.
Remember, as I said before, God didn't ask you to fit IN,
He called you to turn away from SIN (Romans 12:1–21, James 4:4).
You see, God called you out of the darkness to stand OUT,
So that His light can shine through you, then OUT (2 Peter 2:9).
Number 2, you must believe what you READ,
About Jesus and the SEED (John 8:24, John 20:31).
That He was crucified on the CROSS,
And that He died for the LOST (Luke 19:10).
He was buried for three days, then rose from the Dead (Luke 24:7,
     Luke 18:33, Matthew 17:23),
Thus putting the rumors of the Sadducees to BED (Acts 23:8, Mark
     12:18, Luke 20:27–28, Acts 23:8).
For the Sadducees did not believe in the RESURRECTION,
They were the masters of DECEPTION.
Number 3—you must repent—to repent of your past SINS,
That once took control of your heart and soul from WITHIN (Luke
     13:3, Acts 7:30).
Now we come to the verses that all sinners don't CHERISH,
If you don't repent, you will surely PERISH (Luke 13:3, Acts 17:30).
Remember, when you repent with godly sorrow, it brings life BREATH,
But repentance with worldly sorrow brings DEATH (2 Corinthians
     7:10).

Number 4—you must confess—must confess faith in Jesus Christ
before MEN (Romans 10:10),

Then Jesus will acknowledge you before His Father in HEAVEN
(Matthew 10:32–37).

For with his heart, man acknowledges Christ and His RESURRECTION,

And with his mouth, he confesses, resulting in SALVATION (Romans
10:10).

But remember, when you disown Christ before MEN,

He will disown you before His Father in HEAVEN (Matthew 10:32).

Number 5—be baptized—you must be baptized and be born AGAIN,

That is the only way to be free from SIN (John 3:3–5).

Baptism does not clean the dirt from the SKIN,

But cleanses the soul from SIN (2 Peter 3:21, Acts 22:16).

That's right. You are free, at LAST,

From all your sins that controlled your PAST.

Number 6—be faithful—be faithful unto death you are TOLD
(Revelation 2:10),

If you don't, you will have to pay the TOLL (Romans 6:23).

Yes, for the remainder of your life, you must do God's WILL
(Revelation 2:10),

You can't get to heaven by just being STILL.

Those six steps are the plan of SALVATION,

Feel free to do your own EVALUATION.

1. Hear the WORD (Romans 10:17, John 8:31–32).
2. Believe the WORD (Hebrews 11:16, John 20:31).
3. Repent past SINS (Luke 13:3, Acts 7:30).
4. Confess faith in JESUS CHRIST (Romans 10:10, Matthew
   10:32).
5. Be BAPTIZED (Galatians 3:27, Mark 16:16, John 3:3–5,
   Acts 2:38).
6. Be faithful unto DEATH (Revelation 2:10).

And as I try to bring this poem to an END,

I hope that I have influenced you, my FRIEND.

And now, for the moment of truth, did I do my PART?

Did I say something that touched your Heart?
You see, our God is a God of love, and I am here to Tell,
He doesn't want anyone to go to Hell.
For hell is a real place, and God can tell no Lies (Titus 1:2, Hebrews 6:18, Numbers 23:19, 1 Samuel 15:29),
It is a place where the worm never Dies (Mark 9:48).
In the Bible, the word worm is substituted perhaps for Man,
It illustrates the torment that man cannot Stand (Matthew 13:41–42).
It is a constant fire where you are not Consumed (Jude 7, Matthew 18:8),
You will be constantly burning and eternally Doomed (Matthew 3:12, Revelation 14:11).
God is begging you through Me,
Where do you want to spend Eternity?
Can you see what I am doing here Today?
I am pouring out my heart because sin will make you Pay (Romans 6:23).
I have been knowing most of you all for a long Time,
And I consider you'll be good friends of Mine.
I am coming to you with a humble heart and begging, Please,
If you want, I will get on my Knees.
Now I know how an innocent man may Feel,
To be put in jail for something he did not Steal.
He claims his innocence, you See,
But they didn't listen and threw away the Key.
He pleads and talks till he is blue in the Face,
But they look at him with complete Disgrace.
It's like a voice crying out in the wilderness, so hard to Bear,
No one seems to listen; no one seems to Care (John 1:23).
I hope today I have at least planted the Seed (1 Corinthians 3:7, Mark 4:26, Matthew 15:13),
But you must use the Bible as eternal Feed (1 Peter 1:25, 2 Timothy 2:15, Hebrews 4:12, John 5:39).
We pray that the seed that we planted Today (1 Corinthians 3:6–9),
Will take root and show you the Way.

But there is one sin that I forgot to Say,
The sin of pride will make you Pay (Isaiah 2:12, James 4:6).
You see, pride happened to Me (Proverbs 11:2),
And this was one of the sins why Jesus was nailed to the Tree.
You see, people like me don't want to change the volume or change the Tone,
We want to stay in our comfort Zone.
After it's all said and Done,
Pride might be sin number One.
People will be singing the same old Song,
They don't want to admit that their faith is Wrong.
For that was me a long time Ago,
A lost soul, not knowing which way to Go (Luke 19:10).
A few years ago, I was in your Shoes,
I didn't know it, but I was singing the Blues.
For me, Christ was not Around,
But then, there He was, in the Lost And Found.
I found Him in another Church,
I was there, sitting in a pew, like a bird on a Perch.
I was just sitting there, bored, and watching the Clock,
As the minutes went by so slowly, *Tick Tock, Tick Tock*.
But I am here to Say,
That the blood of Christ flows in me each and every Day.
I want to be so full of Christ that if a mosquito bites me and I know that it is just a Bug,
It will fly away, singing. There is power in the Blood.
I am going to end this Story,
Giving your God and my God all the Glory.

Are You Worthy?

Are you worthy of God's Love?
Are you worthy of heaven Above?
Are you worthy when you see a brother or sister on the street corner holding up a Sign?
And you pass them up, not giving them a single Dime (Proverbs 19:17).
Are you worthy when you are watching a movie on TV?
That is filled with cursing and Nudity (Matthew 5:28).
Are you worthy when a good-looking man or woman walks By?
You ponder. Do you want to give them more than just the Eye (Matthew 5:28, 1 John 2:16)?
Are you worthy when you are reading a book that you think is a Must?
While ignoring your Bible that is collecting Dust (Hebrews 4:12).
Are you worthy? Are you worthy of eternal Life?
If you try to covet another man's Wife (Deuteronomy 5:21, Exodus 20:17)?
Are you worthy when you ignore the poor and do that bad Deed?
When it pertains to money, when it pertains to Greed (Proverbs 29:7, 19:17; Psalm 41:1–3)?
Are you worthy? If you love your father and mother more than God?
The answer is no with a Nod (Matthew 10:37).
I ask you: Are you worthy? When you knowingly listen to false teachers and take their Lead,
The answer is: No, do not give them Godspeed (2 John 1:10).
Are you worthy if you don't repent of your SINS?
Jesus says, No, you will die in your Sins. (John 8:24).
Are you worthy if you are not baptized and go Under?
The answer is: No, you will eternally Plunder (John 3:3–5).

I am going to ask you again. Are you worthy if you have not been BAPTIZED?

Read the Bible, not in God's EYES (John 3:5)

Are you worthy if you obey any other doctrine than the one that is in the BIBLE?

The answer is: No, God will hold you ACCOUNTABLE (Galatians 1:8).

Are you worthy if you pray to anyone else but our Lord and SAVIOR?

The answer is: No, you will pay eternally for that kind of BEHAVIOR (1 Timothy 2:5).

Are you worthy if you are constantly having fits of RAGE?

The answer is: No. Read Galatians 5:19 and look at that PAGE.

I ask you. Are you worthy if you do not forgive a sister or a BROTHER?

The answer is: No, you must forgive one ANOTHER (Matthew 6:14–15).

Are you worthy if you have hatred in your HEART?

The answer is: No, sin will not DEPART (1 John 4:20, 1 John3:15)

Are you worthy if you LIE?

The answer is: No, you will eternally DIE (Proverbs 12:22, 6:16–19, 19:5; Deuteronomy 5:20; Leviticus 19:11).

Are you worthy if you are constantly causing arguments in the HOME?

The answer is: No, it is a place where Jesus must ROAM (Galatians 5:20).

Are you worthy if you are constantly taking the name of the Lord our God in VAIN? (Exodus 20:7; Deuteronomy 5:10–11, 6:12–13; Leviticus 19:12)?

The answer is: No, you only have yourself to BLAME (Matthew 5:33–37).

Are you worthy if you don't drink in MODERATION?

The answer is: No, it could hamper your eternal SALVATION (Galatians 5:21).

Are you worthy if you do not acknowledge Jesus before MEN?

The answer is: No, He will not acknowledge you before His Father in HEAVEN (Matthew 10:32).

Are you worthy if you forsake the assembly on the first day of the WEEK?

The answer is: No, you must go and hear God SPEAK (Hebrews 10:25).

Are you worthy if you don't thank God for answering your PRAYERS?

Did you forget, or you just didn't CARE (Psalm 118:21, 66:1–5)?
Are you worthy? Do you ever judge your sister or BROTHER?
The answer is: No, never judge one ANOTHER (Matthew 7:)
Now here is your last question. Are you worthy of HEAVEN?
Or are you just rolling the dice for seven or ELEVEN?
If the dice pop up two, you lose. They call that snake EYES,
And the snake Satan wins with all of his LIES (Genesis 3:4, 2 Corinthians 4:4).
Don't rely on the roll of the dice to determine your FATE,
Act now before it gets too LATE.
Be worthy and repent of your sins TODAY (2 Corinthians 7:10),
And when Jesus comes, He will take you AWAY (1 Thessalonians 4:16–17).
I am going to end this STORY,
By giving God all of the GLORY.

Why Do You Not Listen to Me?

As you read this poem, the appropriate scripture is noted *There*
Please open the Bible so that you can *Compare*
I beg of you: search for the *Truth*
Until you find the *Proof* (James 1:18, Exodus 20:16, Ephesians 6:14, 2 Timothy 2:15, John 8:32)

I do not know why you did not listen to *Me*
It's because of you that my only Son was nailed to a *Tree* (John 3:16, Romans 5:8)
I created everything for you, including the sea and *Land* (Genesis 1:9–10)
And then, on the sixth day, I created *Man*
Didn't I give you enough to *Eat?*
Putting all the food right at your *Feet* (Genesis 1:29, 9:3)
And are you not happy with what I *Did?*
Making it possible that you can be raised from the *Dead* (Romans 8:11, 1 Corinthians 6:14)
And how about getting enough water to *Drink*
Coming out of the ground and from the sky, faster than an eye can *Blink*
Free will is also a gift from *Heaven*
I gave you that and the perfect number *Seven* (Galatians 5:13, John 7:17, Proverbs 16:9)
Let's talk about your body with that special *Design*
Making everyone different is what I had in *Mind*
I formed you in your mother's *Womb*
To live forever and not rest in any man's *Tomb* (Jeremiah 1:5)
I also gave man the seed of *Life*

Making children possible for husband and *Wife* (Genesis 25:21, 1:28)

You will have two eyes—one left and one *Right*

Hopefully, one day you will see the *Light*

The natural light that hits your eyes is easy to *See*

But the light that affects the heart comes from *Me* (Isaiah 60:1; Psalm 27:1, 80:19; 1 Peter 2:9; John 8:12)

So if you walk in the light, as He is in the light, we have fellowship with one *Another*

And the blood of Jesus will purify our sister and our *Brother* (1 John 1:7)

Then there is the heart, which pumps all day and *Night*

Never stopping, not even *Slight*

Just as Jesus cleansed our blood from *Sin*

Our heart cleans our blood from *Within*

Through His blood, we have gained the unmerited favor of God, you *See*

According to His riches for you and *Me* (Ephesians 1:7)

Big decisions, hopefully, are few and far *Apart*

Please follow the Bible and not your *Heart*

Because if you follow your heart every *Day*

It could very possibly lead you *Astray* (Jeremiah 17:9, Matthew 15:19)

Let's talk about your arm, which you can bend at the elbow so that you can *Eat*

Also bends you at the knee so that you can stand on your *Feet*

There is something else that I must mention and *Share*

That I gave you two kidneys and lungs because one day you might need a *Spare*

Now let's talk a little about the virus, which has taken its *Toll*

Affecting some of the young, but mostly the *Old*

This virus hit people so fast that they were not spiritually *Prepared*

Praying to me about their lives being *Spared*

I do not want anyone to be *Lost*

That's why I sent my Son, who died on the *Cross* (2 Peter 3:9)

He came for the young. He came for the *Old*

All He wanted to do was save somebody's *Soul*

You must repent with godly *Sorrow*

And don't procrastinate today and say, I will do it *Tomorrow*
But for *Some*
Tomorrow will never *Come* (Proverbs 27:1, James 4:13–15)
And they will have lost a battle that they could have *Won*
I am asking you with a desperate *Please*
Humble yourself and get on your *Knees* (James 4:10, 2 Chronicles 7:14)
That's right. I am talking to you this *Way*
Because your sins will make you *Pay* (Romans 6:23)
I am going to bring this poem to an *End*
So that we may exalt a brother, sister, relative, or *Friend*
You must do the will of *God*
So that He will look to the right and give you that *Nod* (Matthew 25:33)
Remember this on the day of the Lord: He will come like a thief in the *Night*
With all His angels and with all of His *Might* (1 Thessalonians 5:2–4, Revelation 16:15, Matthew 24:43)
Everyone thinks that they are going to see God when they *Die*
They don't know that they are living a *Lie* (Matthew 7:21)
Ponder this: What would you *Do?*
If Jesus said, I never knew *You*

The Wife of Noble Character
Proverbs 31:10–31

10. A wife of noble character is hard to Find,
    She is worth more than rubies and the best of any Kind.
11. I have full confidence in her all the Time,
    She lacks nothing of value because she is Mine.
12. She brings him good, no harm, no Strife,
    All the days of her Life.
13. She selects wool and flax and always has Plans,
    As she works with those eager Hands.
14. She is like the merchant ship, which brings her food from far Away,
    Nothing will keep her at Bay.
15. She gets up while it is still Night,
    She provides food for the family and servants; she does what is Right.
16. She considers a field and makes it her Own,
    Out of her earnings, she makes a vineyard for the Home.
17. She sets about her work with a lot of Steam,
    Her arms are strong, and they are acting like a Team.
18. She sees that her trading is profitable and doing Alright,
    And her lamp does not go out at Night.
19. In one hand, she holds the distaff and the spindle in the Other,
    Making a ball of yarn for every sister and Brother.
20. She opens her arms to the Poor,
    Helping anyone who comes to her Door.

She extends her hands to those in Need,
Always ready to help and doing a kindly Deed.

21. When it snows, her household has no Fear,
For all of them are clothed in scarlet, which everyone holds so Dear.
22. She is clothed in purple and fine linen and makes covering for her Bed,
Where everyone has a place to lay their Head.
23. Her husband is respected at the city Gate,
Where he sits with the elders to help determine their Fate.
24. She makes linen garments and sells them to the Masses,
And supplies the merchants with Sashes.
25. She is clothed with strength and dignity—this One,
So that she may laugh at the days to Come.
26. She speaks wisdom to Everyone,
And faithful instruction is in her Tongue.
27. She watches over the affairs of her House,
And does not eat the bread of an idle Louse.
28. Her children arise and bless their Mother,
Her husband also arises, gives praise, and doesn't Stutter.
29. Many women do noble things their Way,
But you surpass them all; what can I Say.
30. Charm is deceptive, and beauty just fades Away,
But a woman who fears the Lord is to be praised every single Day.
31. Honor her for all that her hands have Done,
And let her works bring her praise at the city gate to every single One.

The Heart

Why is cancer of the heart so Rare?
Is it because we have a God of compassion, a God of Care?
Let's look at the heart and see what God has to Say,
And why He has kept cancer at Bay.
Let's talk about the heart and the role it Plays,
And how it affects our lives in so many Ways.
Let's check Proverbs 4:23,
And see how the heart affects you and Me.
First of all, above all else, guard your heart and keep it Fit,
For everything you do flows from It.
Now let's look at Proverbs 27:19,
And the way that water works and not to just keep us Clean.
As water reflects the face, and it does its Part,
So one's life reflects the Heart.
Next, listen to Proverbs 10:8,
And you will never be stranded in front of the pearly Gate.
The wise in heart will accept my Commands,
But a chattering fool comes to ruin, ignoring my Demands.
Let's listen to Ezekiel 36:26,
And what it takes to get a heart Fixed.
I will give you a new heart and put a new spirit in you, just like the Rest,
I will remove from you your heart of stone and give you a heart of Flesh.
Next is 1 Peter 3:3–4,
And just listen what God has in Store.
He says that your beauty should not come from the outward adornment and the wearing of Gold,

But let your adorning be hidden in the heart, with the beauty of a
gentle and quiet Soul.
In 1 Samuel 16:7,
God looks at you like a candidate for Heaven.
The Lord said, I do not look at your outward appearance as others
Do,
I look at the heart to find the true You.
Next is Matthew 6:21,
God looks at you as His Son.
For where your treasure is I will Tell,
Your heart will be there as Well.
Next is Proverbs 3:1–2,
Read this verse, and it will tell you what to Do.
It says, Son, keep my commandments in your heart, for they will
prolong your life for many Years,
And it will bring you peace, prosperity, and no shedding of Tears.
Next is David Psalm 90:12, which was written for You,
Read it, for it will also teach You.
It says, Teach us to number our Days,
And that we may gain a heart of wise Ways.
Next is Psalm 19:14,
So that we would read these words and know what they Mean.
It says, May these words of my mouth and the meditation of my
heart be pleasing in your Sight,
To my Lord, my rock, and my redeemer, so that I do what is Right.
Next is Psalm 73:26,
My heart might fail, but God will Fix.
My flesh and my heart may fail Me,
But God is the strength of my heart forever, you See.
The heart has two purposes, not just One,
Because it was made in the image of the Father and of the Son.
Just like the Father created the World,
And the Son saved the World.
Now the physical heart purifies the blood for the young and Old,
While the spiritual heart regenerates the Soul.
The physical heart remembers God, made with a Nod,

And the spiritual heart is made to guide us from INSIDE.
The spiritual heart has a certain feeling deep INSIDE,
And no matter how hard you try, you cannot HIDE.
A spiritual heart will love to hear a bird SING,
Then will cry its eyes out when the bird has a broken a WING.
A spiritual heart will unfold the grace of God when we PRAY,
Not just once in a while, but every single DAY.
A spiritual heart is there to show you love, pity, and SORROW,
For yesterday, today, and TOMORROW.
So when you are down and out and things aren't going your WAY,
Think about your physical heart that beats over one hundred thou-
    sand times a DAY.
And remember that your spiritual heart is the gateway to your SOUL,
And whatever you feed it, that will be you when you get OLD.
Sometimes the spiritual heart sees what is invisible to the EYE,
It touches your inner soul and makes you want to CRY.
A true friend is what the spiritual heart needs all the TIME,
It brings out the light and makes things SHINE.
Let my soul smile through my heart and my heart smile through my
    EYES,
That I may bring spiritual riches that never ever DIES.
And finally, and most importantly, Jesus will make a spiritual heart
    His HOME,
A permanent residence, where He will never ever ROAM.
For you see, God gave us a heart to preach the gospel with LOVE,
To convince and convict people about our God from up ABOVE.
And this is what God wants me to DO,
To pass the gospel on to YOU, YOU, and YOU,
I am going to end this poem and story by giving God all the GLORY.

The Sheep and the Goats

This poem is about Matthew 25:31–46,
Ponder on these verses slowly, and you will receive a spiritual Fix.
It tells you how the Son of Man shall come in all of His Glory,
And you will understand when you hear all of the Story.
And all of His angels will come with Him as Well,
Because they too shall sit upon the throne and might have a story to Tell.
Then everyone will stand before Him,
And He will decide who did good and who did Sin.
He will separate one from Another,
Judging every sister and Brother.
He will separate the sheep from the goats that Day,
And if you are a goat, you better begin to Pray.
He will put the sheep on the right and the goats on the Left Side,
You will know then what Jesus did Decide.
Then the king will say to those on the Right,
Come, you who are blessed by Father, claim your inheritance Tonight.
For I was hungry, and you gave me something to Eat,
And I was thirsty, and you put the water bottle at my Feet.
I was a stranger, and you invited me into your Homes,
And I needed clothes, and you clothed my naked Bones.
I was sick, and you looked after me. What could I Say?
I was in prison, and you came to visit me every single Day.
Then the righteous answered, Lord, we don't remember doing these things Today,
But we will certainly want to hear what you have to Say.
The king will reply, "I tell you the truth. Whatever you did for your brother, you See,

You did it for Me."
Then He will say to those on His left, "Depart from me. You are
cursed into the eternal Fire,"
"Prepare yourself for the devil. You sinner and Liar."
"For I was hungry, and you gave me nothing to Eat,"
"You didn't even throw a bone at my Feet."
"For I was thirsty, and you gave me nothing to Swallow,"
"I was thirsty like an old dying tree, empty and Hollow."
"I was a stranger with no home and no clothes to Wear,"
"You didn't even look at me. You didn't even Care."
"Then I was sick, and what did you Do?"
"Put me on the back burner, like cooking a Stew."
They will answer, "Lord, when did we see you hungry, thirsty, or a
stranger in Need,"
"If it was you, Lord, we would have done that good Deed."
The king replied, "I tell you the truth. Whatever you did not do for
your brother, you See,"
"You did not do it for Me."
Then they will go away to eternal punishment and be Lost,
But the righteous to eternal life because they obeyed the Cross.
I will now end this poem and Story,
By giving God all the Glory.

The Way of the Seed

First, let's give God all the GLORY
Without Him, there would not be a STORY
That's right. Thank God for the sixth DAY
Without it, we would not be here TODAY (Genesis 1:27–31)

This poem was written for those who study the Bible and practice it
    Too
God, have mercy on those who don't have a CLUE
I think it is important that we must UNDERSTAND
That when God made us, He had a PLAN

According to Jeremiah 1:5
God knew you before you were ALIVE
In Ephesians 1:4
He chose us in Him before the creation of the world
Could we ask for anything MORE?

In Ephesians 1:5, in God's love, He predestined us to be ADOPTED
As His sons, through Jesus Christ, with His will and PLEASURE
Something that we must always TREASURE
This is God's plan of PREDESTINATION (Romans 8:11)
Not God's IMAGINATION (Romans:28–30)

For God made heaven and earth in six days so that He could RULE
    (Genesis 1)
Resting on the seventh day, using the earth as His FOOTSTOOL
    (Genesis 2:2)

He breathes life into Adam, and out of Adam, He took a rib to make
    Eve (Genesis 2:22)
Making Eve his companion so that she can CONCEIVE (Genesis
    2:18–20)

To populate the earth—that was God's PLAN (Genesis 1:26–28)
Although He could have done it by just waving His HAND
So Adam took Eve as his MATE
And did God's will and started to POPULATE (Genesis 1:26–28)

We are going fast forward, if that's OKAY
For God's plan cannot be held at BAY
God told Noah to build an ARK (Genesis 6:14, 22)
And Noah did God's will and did not complain or BARK.

Then it rained for forty days and forty NIGHTS (Genesis 7:12)
Everything was killed—everything in their SIGHTS.
We jump now to the father of NATIONS (Genesis 17:5)
Where Abraham plays a part in God's plan of CREATION

For God made a covenant with ABRAHAM
That his future generations will be on HAND
When He gives them the promise LAND (Genesis 17:4–8)
God also told Abraham that in one year he would be blessed with a
    SON (Genesis 18:9–12)
His wife Sarah laughed and said, I am ninety. How can this be DONE?
    (Genesis 21:1–7)

Well, God made His promise come TRUE
Even though Sarah was about a year from NINETY-TWO (Genesis
    21:1–7)
Isaac was his NAME
And he will have a son who will bring Israel to FAME
He was Jacob, who was next in God's PLAN
He would have twelve sons who would divide up the promised LAND
Revelation 7:4–8

This brings us to Judah, Jacob's fourth Son
Far out of his seed, the Son of God will Come (Matthew 1:1–3)
Now Er was Judah's firstborn, but he was wicked in God's Sight
So the Lord put him to death one Night (Genesis 38:6–7)

Then Judah told his second son, Onan, to lie with Tamar Er's Wife
To fulfill his brother-in-law duty and bring forth Life (Genesis 38:8–10)
But Onan did not consummate the Deed
Because he failed to fertilize the Seed (Genesis 38:9–10)

So Onan was now wicked in God's Sight
And he did not survive the Night (Genesis 38:9–10)
His third son, Shelah, did not marry Tamar Either
For Judah feared this son would also get the Ether (Genesis 38:11)

But as you know, Tamar tricked Judah to get his Seed
And the baby she had, to Jesus, did Lead (Genesis 39:12–26)
This goes to show you that when God has a Plan
He is going to make it work with the last-standing Man

To the fact that no one can Deny
That Er and Onan did Die (Genesis 38:6–10)
Imagine if you were there to be a witness to all these Guys
The plan of God unfolds before your very Eyes

On second thought, we are sitting here right now and worshiping on this Land
We are God's Plan
In Ephesians 2:11, Paul says it really Nice
We are all one in Christ (Ephesians 2:11–13)

Because of Him

The following things I am going to list Here,
Are things about our Lord and Savior that I want you to Hear.
Because of Him, who died on the Cross,
He came for the sinners. He came for the Lost (Luke 5:32).
Because of Him, who died on the cross and took our Place,
It came from Jesus, who gave us truth and Grace (John 1:17).
Because of Him, we were buried by baptism into Death,
And we will be raised from the dead with eternal Breath (Romans 6:4).
Because of Him, the Bible says that you will have no fear when you Die (Psalm 23:4),
That is written in the Bible, and the Bible will never ever Lie (Numbers 23:19).
Because of Him, we have no guilt about our Past,
He has cleansed us of our sins from the first to the Last (1 John 1:9).
Because of Him, who has something in Store,
That He will remember our sins no More (Hebrews 8:12).
Because of Him, we are reconciled with our father in Heaven,
Not just rolling the dice, hoping for a seven or Eleven (Romans 5:10).
Because the sins of man have alienated God from Us,
But the death of His Son has made us righteous and Just (Colossians 1:20–23).
Because of Him, Jesus is the mediator of the new covenant, you See,
And He says no one comes to the Father except through Me (John 14:6).
Because of Him, He is the atoning sacrifice for our sins, and not only for ours but also for the sins of the World,

Including every man, woman, boy, and GIRL (1 John 2:2).

Because of Him, we have been set free from SIN,

And become slaves of righteousness and have a chance for HEAVEN (Romans 6:6).

Because of Him, salvation is found in no one else's NAME,

And He is the only one who can bring you to the ETERNAL FLAME (Acts 4:12).

Because of Him, He laid down His life for Us,

He died for sinners. He died for the UNJUST (Romans 5:6–8).

Because of Him, He rendered the devil powerless with His last BREATH,

And He condemned him to hell to ETERNAL DEATH (Hebrews 2:14–15).

Because of Him, He demonstrated the greatest act of LOVE,

By dying for His friends while being sent from ABOVE (John 15:13).

Because of Him, He reconciled the Jew and Gentile as ONE,

He did it so that God's will would be DONE (Ephesians 2:11–16).

Because He died on the cross, He humbled Himself before MAN,

But none of His people could quite UNDERSTAND (Philippians 2:8).

Because of Him, He canceled our debt to SIN,

What a terrible position we were IN (Colossians 2:14).

Because of Him, He fulfilled the prophecy of a long time AGO,

And it was recorded in the Bible so that everyone would KNOW (Psalm 22:14–18, Isiah 53:4–7, Zechariah 12:10).

Read and believe these truths that are in the BIBLE,

Because of Him, we would all be held LIABLE.

Remember, it's only eighteen inches from head to heart, so let's get them TOGETHER,

So that we can be in heaven FOREVER.

Hell

The trip originates at the gates of the second DEATH (Revelation 21:8),
The air is different. I can barely catch my BREATH.
As I pass through the doorway, I am heading away from the LIGHT,
The further I go, the more it seems to be NIGHT.
With each passing moment, the darkness becomes more INTENSE (Matthew 25:30),
What am I doing here? It doesn't make any SENSE.
Now the darkness becomes more EXTREME,
I am really scared now and ready to SCREAM.
All of a sudden, there is no light that I can SEE,
Just utter darkness—that terrifies ME (Matthew 25:30).
I have a constant sense of FRIGHT,
As if something is lurking in the vail of the NIGHT.
Whatever it is, it is just there, producing fear like I have never known BEFORE,
I am now panicking, trying to find an open DOOR.
But to no AVAIL,
It is like being in a black JAIL.
No matter where I go, the intensity of the darkness is all AROUND (Matthew 25:30),
It is only matched by the intensity of any joyful SOUND.
There is no laughter, no music, no sound to HEAR,
No sound seems to penetrate my inner EAR.
As I move further, I hear faint sounds of moaning, wailing, and SCREAMS,
I pinched myself. Am I having nightmares and bad DREAMS (Matthew 13:42)?

Now these sounds seem to be coming through the dark from every DIRECTION,
Am I here because of heaven's REJECTION?
In the distance, I see a faint light. It flickers like a FLAME,
Could I be in hell? I call out to Jesus and His holy NAME.
But no answer do I GET,
I fall down on my knees, trembling and UPSET.
All of a sudden, I am pushed to my feet by a hot, burning WIND,
Searing my eyes and burning my CHIN (Luke 16:24).
It's right at the edge of unbearable, hot, searing, intolerable HEAT (Isaiah 33:14),
Piercing my inner body and melting my FEET (Mark 9:43).
For my body seems to be on fire all OVER (Revelation 20:15),
Please let me die so that I can have some CLOSURE.
But God told us the truth: He cannot LIE (Hebrews 6:18),
Hell is a place where the worm will never DIE (Mark 9:48).
I still can't believe that I am HERE,
Where are all of my friends whom I thought would be NEAR?
All of a sudden, I stumbled on a group of others whom I didn't KNOW,
I told them that I was lost and asked which way to GO.
As they opened their mouths, no words came OUT,
I was getting really frustrated with them, and I started to SHOUT.
Then one of them made a weeping and wailing SOUND (Matthew 13:50),
When I heard that, I collapsed to the GROUND.
For it was true what the Bible had SAID,
That I was in hell, and I was DEAD.
Then I saw others who were gashing their teeth as if they were in some invisible PAIN (Matthew 13:50),
All that I was saying was, Please give me some RAIN (Luke 16:24).
How I wish I could send a message to those whom I left BEHIND (Luke 16:26–28),
Giving them a signal or some kind of SIGN (Luke 16:26–28).
I wish I could warn them about this PLACE (Luke 16:26–28),
No joy, no peace, no goodness—just utter DISGRACE.

I can't think back to that day when I made the decision to come
    HERE,
Of my rejection of Christ, who was so DEAR (Isaiah 53:3).
I find myself hoping that my loved ones don't come HERE,
Seeing my children would be my greatest FEAR.
Speaking of my children, I miss them so MUCH,
Not able to hug, hold, kiss, or even TOUCH.
When we went on vacation, we would have an itinerary to see what
    we had planned AHEAD,
Unfortunately for this trip, there is none for I am DEAD.
For the first time since I arrived, I began to sense the great gulf that
    is fixed between me and GOD (Luke 16:26),
I am looking for a boat to take on the outgoing TIDE.
But there is none NOWHERE,
Only this constant heat that my spirit cannot BEAR (Revelation
    20:15).
Through the darkness, I see a new face walking my WAY,
I see the terror in his eyes, of him not knowing what to SAY.
He told me that he was lost and asked me to show him the WAY,
I tried to open my mouth, but my throat was so dry that I could not
    TALK,
I could not even open my mouth. My saliva tasted like CHALK.
I strained to talk but could not make a PEEP,
Then finally, the sound that I made was that of a WEEP.
Are you kidding me? I am now one of them. What can I SAY?
I can't believe that I have only been here one DAY.
It's hard to comprehend this one-day JOURNEY,
That seems like an ETERNITY.
All of a sudden, I hear someone knocking at the DOOR,
I jump out of bed, and it's my neighbor Bob, who lives next DOOR.
Is this for real? This has all been a DREAM,
It's funny—how real all of this can SEEM.
But do any of us really know how it is in HELL?
No one has ever come back to us to TELL.
But God has left us a book that has a list of DETAILS,
How man succumbs to the ways of the world and FAILS.

I am so happy that it was just a dream, and it's not too LATE,
To change our lives, that will determine our FATE.
For Jesus did His part. He saved our SOUL,
So that one day we might become WHOLE.
For you see, we were just sinners saved by GRACE,
We stood condemned to death, and He took our PLACE.
He fought our battle that caused His DEATH,
He won our battle; that gave us BREATH.
For you see, He was the perfect lamb of God that was SLAIN,
We must do our part so that He does not die in VAIN.
So you see, this was just a DREAM,
We have time to get on God's TEAM.
He will take you when you are young. He will take you when you're
    OLD,
All He wants to do is save your SOUL.
So be alive in Christ TODAY,
And let's have it His WAY.
I would like to end this STORY,
By giving God all the GLORY.

Transformation

Before we get into our topic of TRANSFORMATION,
The Bible (God) is going to make a DECLARATION.
For the message of the cross is foolishness to those who are PERISHING,
But to those chosen who are being saved, the power of God is very
  CHERISHING (1 Corinthians 1:18).
Through the gospel message of Christ, we learn to TRANSFORM,
Your former life of corrupted DESIRES,
Into the likeness of God—a likeness that He ADMIRES (Ephesians
  4:22–24, Colossians 3:10).
The biggest change in a Christian's LIFE,
Is that you are transformed to be like CHRIST (2 Corinthians 2:18,
  Romans 12:2).
Full transformation doesn't happen right AWAY,
But slowly, day by DAY.
That's right. You are changing, you SEE,
And the Holy Spirit is in you, and the Holy Spirit is in ME (Acts
  2:38, 5:32; Ephesians 1:13–14; Luke 12:12; John 14:15–17).
We are going to talk about some things that are no longer THERE,
That have been taken out of your life by a God of CARE (Job 1:21).
First of all, sinful habits have plagued you and have caused you noth-
  ing but STRIFE (Hebrews 13:6, Romans 12:2, Mark 7:20–23),
Then all of a sudden, they were dropped from your LIFE.
They have been dropped from your HEART,
With little or no effect on your PART.
Things that used to entertain you years AGO,
Are now out of your life, they just had to Go.
But some changes are FAST,

And God takes people out of your life so that these changes will Last
(1 Corinthians 5:13, Psalms 119:29).
That is what our God is doing for You,
And if you read the Bible, you will find that out Too.
Little by little, He takes people out of your life whom you don't
Need (1 Corinthians 5:13),
Because He knows you cannot grow by using bad Seed (Matthew
13:24–30, Matthew 7:18).
You see, He wants you to be nurtured in good Soil (Luke 8:15,
Matthew 13:23),
To be able to conquer Satan, who tries to deceive us All (John 8:44).
The people that you felt good about being Around,
You look at them in a different light, and they are nowhere to be
Found (Job 1:21).
The same people that you shared the darkness with are no longer
There,
They were taken out of your life by a God of love—a God of Care
(1 Corinthians 5:13).
God wants you rid of these people who bring you Down,
He wants you to grow spiritually strong and spiritually Sound (1
Corinthians 2:14, Colossians 1:9–10).
Food and drink you used to like and thought had a great Taste,
God has taken them out of your life as garbage and Waste (Job 1:21).
The shows on TV have also changed, you See,
What you used to watch that was rated R is now rated PG.
Next, the Bible says that you will be justified by your Words,
And you will be condemned by those Words (Matthew 12:36–37).
The words that you speak are suddenly purified and seasoned with
Grace (Colossians 3:8, Ephesians 4:29),
The people around you can't believe what has taken Place (Matthew
5:15–16).
The words used were harsh and crude by the Sender,
Now these words are soft and Tender.
That's right. People around you will see the Change,
They will say, What's up? He is acting mighty Strange.
Even some of them will change how they Act,

It is out of respect for you, and that's a Fact.
And sometimes, as you walk toward the other Guys,
They stop telling dirty jokes and Lies.
You have a different outlook toward others than Before,
Your love and compassion are growing more and More (2 Corinthians
    5:17).
You have changed. It's not all about you, you See,
For the Holy Spirit who now is in you and is in Me (1 Corinthians
    6:19–20, John 14:16, John 14:26, Romans 5:5).
These miracles that happened in your life are God-Given,
You can now take on the name Christian.
For you see, the first six letters in Christian make up Christ. You have
    been cleansed and made Whole,
It is God Almighty working on your very Soul.
Please remember, if this touches your heart in any Way,
Don't forget to get on your knees and Pray.
For your heavenly Father wants you to go to heaven Too,
He is waiting for a godly Thank-You.
I am going to end this Story,
By giving God all the Glory.

Ten Words to Ponder

There are two phrases that we are going to discuss Here,
One you might say one day, and one you don't want to Hear.
Both of these phrases combined only have ten words, you See,
Ten most powerful words for you and Me.
I know you are probably wondering what these ten words can Be,
I will give you a hint. They pertain to your Eternity.
You see, more people go through their lives spending more time worrying about their Vacation,
Than planning for their eternal Salvation.
And the best part about this is that I get it. I Understand,
I was almost like every one of you, down to the very last Man.
That's right. I said, "I have to work and support my kids and Wife."
I wasn't thinking about my salvation or eternal Life.
Add to this: the cares of the world are pulling God away from Us,
And it makes it harder to be righteous and Just.
Remember, if you hear these words on judgment Day,
Then you will know that hell is on the Way.
Here is your next clue. There are seven words in the first phrase, you See,
And in the second phrase, there are only Three.
Ten words in All,
Three bring life, the other seven make you Fall.
And on judgment day, this is going to happen to all of Us,
We are going to stand before God, and He will tell us if we were righteous and Just.
I know that it is hard to believe, guys, that there is such a Place,
But you will see Jesus Face-to-Face.
I would like to know: How would you feel, and what would you Do?

If you heard these seven words: "DEPART FROM ME, I NEVER KNEW YOU" (Matthew 7:21–23).

What would you do, and how would you FEEL?

You couldn't do anything. Your fate would be SEALED.

Act now to determine your FATE,

And say these three words before it's too LATE.

For starters, you must say these three words. Don't keep them at BAY,

Say them with a humble heart; say them TODAY.

Say these three words, and we pray that the devil will FLEE,

These three words are "LORD, SAVE ME."

Reach out and grab the Lord's HAND,

He would like to save everyone, down to the very last MAN.

Take control of your life Now,

And when Jesus comes, you will be ready to Bow.

Remember this. We all let weeds grow in our field, where once there was WHEAT,

Take control now—sins and devils, you will DEFEAT.

You want to stay ALIVE,

Open the Bible. Read and do John 3:5.

I am going to end this STORY,

By giving God all the GLORY.

The Cross

Over two thousand years ago, Jesus died on the CROSS,
He died for sinners. He died for the LOSS (Luke 19:10).
When He died on the cross, He took our PLACE,
So that we could be saved—saved by His GRACE (Ephesians 2:8–9).
Let's go back before His DEATH,
And see how the sins of man took His last BREATH (Romans 5:6–8).

His ministry started in the city of GALILEE (Matthew 3:13),
Where He told Peter and Andrew to follow THEE (Matthew 4:18–23).
He told Peter and Andrew, I will make you fishers of MEN (Matthew 4:19),
Then Jesus went on to pick the remaining TEN (Matthew 10:1–4).
There were twelve apostles in ALL (Luke 6:12–16),
And the thirteenth one was named PAUL.

These were not doctors or lawyers. They were fishermen and tentmakers who had a story to TELL (Matthew 4:18–22, Acts 18:1–4),
About the greatness of heaven or the torments of HELL (Luke 16:24).
Let's take a look back at that tragic DAY (Matthew 13:42, Matthew 25:41),
And wondered what God would have to SAY.

I remember Him when He was just a baby and a FIRSTBORN,
Then I watched them hammer in thorn after THORN (John 19:2–5).
I remember watching my Son sleep at NIGHT,
Then I watched them hit Him with all their MIGHT (Mark 15:19).
I remember when I looked at my baby boy, so tiny and FRAIL,

49

Then I watched as they hammered in nail after NAIL (Mark 15:26,
Acts 2:23).
As my Son's life hung in the balance between good and evil on the
CROSS,
One life went to paradise; one life was a LOSS (Luke 23:32–55).
This represents every man and woman on EARTH,
To believe in Jesus and seek His CHURCH.

It was a terrible thing that happened to my SON,
But my plan had to be DONE.
You see, He was hung on a tree in utter DISGRACE (Deuteronomy
21:23),
And by His death, I have given you GRACE.
Remember, He died for the sins of the WORLD (1 John 2:2),
Every man, every woman, every boy, and every GIRL.
You have a memory like MINE,
The only thing is that mine is DIVINE (2 Peter1:3–4, Romans 1:20).

But it is similar to the one that I gave YOU,
And I will never forget what they put my Son THROUGH.
It's all over now, and for those who repented with godly sorrow, I will
remember their sins no MORE (2 Corinthians 7:10, Jeremiah
31:34),
But the ones who did not repent, we know what's in STORE (Luke
13:3).
The same thing is going to happen to anyone who doesn't listen to
ME,
Hell is their DESTINY.
For the false teachers, I can't stomach you SEE (2 Peter 2)
Hell is their DESTINY (Galatians 1:7–8).

But today, we celebrate the glorious resurrection of my one and only
SON,
He did this for each and every ONE.
Please never forget my Son's PLIGHT,
For because of Him, you have everlasting LIFE (1 John 5:11).

Light that will shine for ETERNITY,

Light that will eliminate hell as your DESTINY (John 3:16, Isaiah 60:20).

To conclude, He came. He lived. He died to save our SOULS,

So that one day His story would be TOLD.

So when you are in the dark and turn on the LIGHT,

Always remember, your Lord and Savior, with all of the pain, and all of His PLIGHT.

Remember, Jesus died on the cross to show you the WAY (1 Peter 3:18),

So that you would be with Him one DAY.

For the way to the heart of our Lord and SAVIOR,

Depends on our human BEHAVIOR (Romans 14:13).

For we know that Jesus died, was buried, and now has RISEN,

Just like every one of us when we were baptized and became CHRISTIANS.

And now, what we all must do, my FRIEND,

Is for us to endure to the END (Matthew 10:22–23).

If we can all agree to do this with a NOD,

Then yes, we will be in heaven with almighty GOD.

And I will end this poem and STORY,

By giving God all the GLORY.

Are You in a Hurry?

Hurry is of the devil, you SEE,
Love is from Jesus for you and for ME.
Slow is the speed of LOVE,
Compare it to that of a white, loving DOVE.
Love has the inner speed of God from ABOVE,
Because God is the speed of LOVE.
Love is compatible with peace and JOY,
It is there for every man, woman, girl, and BOY.
Paul describes love as patience in the HEART,
True love that will never ever DEPART.
If you are in a hurry, let me just MENTION,
Remember, you cannot get God's ATTENTION.
You see, hurry is the death of a PRAYER,
Either you don't know that, or you really just don't CARE.
Always remember that if you walk with Jesus, it's like a slow breeze and WIND,
If you walk in the world, it's like a long journey that will never END.
For starters, everyone out there is trying to get your attention, like Facebook and TWITTER,
Trying to get your business, go to the highest BIDDER.
That's right. Let's talk about Facebook, Twitter, and your cell phone, which take up a lot of your TIME,
Doing nothing constructive, just playing ONLINE.
Let's face it. We are all hooked on Facebook, Twitter, and the PHONE,
And believe me, we are not ALONE.
The digital age was at our front DOOR,
And we opened it, and it's going to be more, more, and MORE.
The above-mentioned things take time out of our LIFE,

It's called a hurry sickness that can cause nothing but stress and
     STRIFE.
Now get this: hurry is a form of violence on the SOUL,
It can cause you to be restless and irritable if the truth is TOLD.
Your priorities are out of order because of your LIFESTYLE,
Slow down, relax, and take a breath for a WHILE.
Hurry can cause emotional numbness, and you wonder if you are
     SANE,
And not be able to feel another person's PAIN.
Hurry can make your body tired, so you don't feel your SOUL,
And do the spiritual things that God has TOLD.
Hurry will make you isolated and disconnected from the one ABOVE,
You know who He is. Our God of LOVE.
Hurry kills relationships that people HAVE,
Because love takes time that hurry does not HAVE.
It's important that we are aware of our everyday LIVES,
So that we can take steps to spiritually SURVIVE.
Every day, so many people live without a sense of God's PRESENCE,
Not having that inner feeling, not knowing God's ESSENCE.
We are oblivious to God around US,
The only one who is righteous and JUST.
Our God is there for you every DAY,
But you must set aside enough time to ponder and PRAY.
Remember, your mind is the portal to your SOUL,
And what you fill it with will shape your character, whether you are
     young or OLD.
In the end, your life is no more than the sum of what you gave your
     attention TO,
Listen to me. Every word of this poem is TRUE.
In other words, when you are on your death bed, you will look back
     and REALIZE,
That you have wasted your one chance, and your eternal happiness
     will not MATERIALIZE.
What good is it for someone to gain the whole world yet forfeit your
     SOUL,
This pertains to everyone, whether you're young or OLD.

Does this sound like someone you know? Am I walking on your
TOES?
Is this your life? Only you and God KNOWS.
Is it possible? Could this be God talking to YOU?
This could be your chance, so what are you going to DO?
Are you going to keep on doing it and get what you DESERVE?
Or are you going to man up? Do you have the NERVE?
Don't tell me that you need more time. That's not the SOLUTION,
You're living in a world that's full of spiritual POLLUTION.
The solution is to take control of your life and slow DOWN,
If you don't, you will be hell BOUND.
Can you imagine being made in the image of GOD?
He made you out of dust and a loving NOD.
We have limitations. Listen, you can't do it ALL,
We have limitations that can cause us to STALL.
You see, our bodies can only be in one PLACE,
We may never have a chance to complete this RACE.
Next, our minds are LIMITED,
We don't know what we don't KNOW.
Our personalities and emotions also play a role in the limitations of
our LIVES,
It is what gives us our fortitude, and it gives us our DRIVES.
Next, our origin also plays a PART,
Did our parents raise us with a loving HEART?
Our social and economic origins also play a ROLE,
Generations of poverty can take their TOLL.
Next, education comes into PLAY,
Did they finish grammar school or high school? Did they go all the
WAY?
The next limitation is our LIFESTYLE,
Was it filled with caring for the elderly or caring for a CHILD?
All of the above limitations that we have mentioned so FAR,
Have molded our lives, and that's who we ARE.
We find God's will for our lives in our LIMITATIONS,
But time is our main LIMITATION.
It's time that I bring this poem to an END,

And I hope that you have learned something, my FRIEND.
There is a whole lot more that I can SAY,
But you see, I am running out of time TODAY.
I am going to end this STORY,
By giving God all the GLORY.

Lonely Is the Brave

Do we know how it feels to be alone and trapped at Home?
Being unable to see your family and unable to Roam.
Lonely is the Brave,
Just you and four walls is like being trapped in a Cave.

Now I know how a prisoner feels being confined to his Cell,
It's a sad and lonely world. I am here to Tell.
Sometimes I sit in my chair and think about the Past,
And how life just goes by so very, very Fast.

Now I know how it feels to be in Jail,
It's like just sitting around, trying to make Bail.
The only thing that makes it easy for me to Bear,
Is that I am not going to get the electric Chair.

Life is too ironic to fully Understand,
All we can do is be a part of God's Plan.
This is how it goes. It takes noise to appreciate Silence,
Sadness to recognize Happiness,
And Absence to value Presence.

You see, God gives us trials for a Reason,
To prepare us season after Season.
I think loneliness can be a part of the mortal experience when you
    get Old,
And God wants you to search for your inner Soul.

You see, God wants you to be COMPLETE,
When you humble yourself at His FEET.
You see, God doesn't want you to ponder sin in the PAST,
He wants you to live each day as if it were the LAST.

Because after all is said and DONE,
Tomorrow is promised to no ONE.
We live in a world today that is pulled apart in every DIRECTION,
We need solitude for a time of REFLECTION.

So when you are all alone and down and don't know what to DO,
Just remember, God will never forsake YOU.
For He is a God of love and a God of CARE,
And for you, He will always be THERE.
And I would like to end this poem and STORY,
By giving God all the GLORY.

The Storm

We are going through a storm that we cannot see
A storm that affects you, a storm that affects me
No one knows how it started. No one can tell
We know it started in China, making this world a living hell
Then it went to Italy, we are told
Infiltrating the Italian cities and killing off the old
Then this storm entered Washington State and New York City
Causing sickness and death, isn't it a pity?
This storm is now in our city, gaining up steam
Is this really happening, or is this a bad dream?
It's time that America and the rest of the world wake up so that the real story can be told
That this is our God, who is in full control
This storm that was sent to break you
Is going to be the storm God uses to make you
It is time that we look at this virus as our storm and rain
Having God in our hearts will keep us sane
So here we are, quarantined in our homes
Away from that deadly virus that roams
What can we do? What can we say?
There is nothing that will keep this virus at bay
Let's look to the Bible for the solution
This world is full of people, sickness, evil, and pollution
People are polluted with lust, hatred, rage, envy, and greed
We are to look to the Bible to take heed
In John 16:33, Jesus tells us that we don't live in a bubble
But that we live in a world where we will have trouble
But take this to heart, every man, woman, boy, and girl

He will overcome this world

And in John 17:24–26, Jesus says, "Father, I want those that you have given me to be with me where I am, that they may see My glory and behold"

I am the savior of their very soul

Let's look to our Lord and Savior

For He is in tune with our human behavior

At this time, I would like to say a prayer

Letting the world know that our God really does care

And for everyone to open their eyes

And believe that the Bible tells no lies

If you read the Bible very slow,

It will tell you what you want to know

In Luke 13:3, Jesus says you will perish if you do not repent

So it is time that the whole world honor God and His Son that He has sent

In John 3:5, Jesus says that in order to enter the kingdom of God, you must be baptized

Why is this so hard for people to realize?

1 Timothy 2:5 says that there is only a mediator between God and man

Why is this so hard for people to understand?

When they pray, they should say prayers to no other one

Than to God the Son

A few weeks ago, corona, to me, meant a part of the sun

Now this corona has everyone on the run

God gave us one sun that gives off light

God gave us His Son, who is the light

God wants you to do what is right

Read and obey the Bible like you know you should

And He will bring you through this storm like you knew He would

Truth

First of all, the earth is traveling at sixty-seven thousand miles an hour around the sun. Do you believe THAT?
You better, because that is a FACT.
Now the moon is traveling forward at that same SPEED,
While at the same time revolving around the earth, I know it's hard to CONCEIVE.
Did you know that eighty percent of the earth's oxygen comes from the OCEAN?
It happened when God got that NOTION.
The other twenty percent comes from trees, you SEE,
I would never lie; that wouldn't be ME.
Let's talk about the elbow, and we think it is really NEAT,
If we didn't have one, we couldn't EAT.
God also gave a bending knee to every MAN,
Without that knee, you could not get up to STAND.
God also gave you that knee for another REASON,
To bow for His Son, who could return any time, any SEASON.
He also gave us two lungs and two kidneys, one for a SPARE,
Because He is a God of love, a God of CARE.
He is a God like no OTHER,
We are able to use a kidney or lung donated by a sister or a BROTHER.
He also gave us eyes to see all of His GLORY,
And a mind to comprehend and understand this STORY.
Next are the eyelids, which are very UNIQUE,
Without them, you would never get any SLEEP.
Now we have eyelashes, which are a MUST,
They filter out particles of dirt and DUST.
The eyebrows catch the sweat and make it run down the SIDES,

Keeping rain and sweat out of your EYES.
Now your lips play a ROLE,
They would be the gateway to your SOUL.
You see your lips make words that people HEAR,
They can make them feel joy or bring them to a TEAR.
Then He gave us a HEART,
To pump blood that reaches every PART.
He gave us fingers and a HAND,
So that we can make castles in the SAND.
Let's talk about the toes on your feet that thrust your body forward
     when you WALK,
They make you run faster so that you will get home before it gets
     DARK.
All these things MENTIONED,
Were given to us with divine INTENTION.
They were given to us by God up ABOVE,
Because He is a God of LOVE.
I would like to end this STORY,
By giving God all the GLORY.

Our Heavenly Father

Here we are, heavenly Father, the church that your Son died for, one church for ALL,
A powerful church, waiting for your CALL.
This church was made from top to bottom by Your DESIGN,
We follow the Bible. We walk the LINE.
But this world that we live in pulls us AWAY,
And it is so hard to keep the devil at BAY.
You see, the devil is like a roaring lion, looking for someone to DECEIVE,
Just like in the garden of Eden, like Adam and EVE (1 Peter 5:8–9).
Now the world celebrates Father's Day TODAY,
But we celebrate our heavenly Father every DAY.
You see, heavenly Father, every second that goes BY,
Because of you, we either live or DIE.
Because of you, heavenly Father, we see the stars in the heavens at NIGHT,
Because of you, we see a beautiful sunset—what a SIGHT!
Because of you, heavenly Father, we give thanks for every MEAL,
For the food that you provided us and that we didn't have to STEAL.
Thank you, heavenly Father, for the roof over our HEAD,
And providing us with a nice, clean BED.
Thank you, heavenly Father, for those children and grandchildren—those precious little girls and GUYS.
One look at them brings tears to our EYES.
Our heavenly Father, you did not stop THERE,
You are a God of love, a God of CARE.
Thank you so much, heavenly Father, for what you have DONE,
By giving us your one and only SON.

We praise you for all these things and so much MORE,
And we come to you every day as our Father and Lord, whom we
    ADORE.
Heavenly Father, we find rest and peace in you alone. We give you
    PRAISE,
For giving us strength in these trying DAYS.
We are going to end this poem in a very special WAY,
By wishing that YOU have a heavenly, divine Father's DAY.

Are You Ready?

In the game of life and the Super Bowl game, it comes down to one WAY,
You must be ready for that game and judgment DAY.
The similarities are plain to SEE,
They pertain to you and ME.
The Super Bowl is played on a SUNDAY,
We go to church on SUNDAY.
Every professional football team is owned by one MAN,
Our team has God, who is the Father of the Son of MAN.
Every team has a coach who tries to inspire his men and make them feel like they BELONG.
We have a preacher who guides and leads us in SONG.
The players are issued a playbook, for which they are held LIABLE,
We, too, have a playbook. They call it the BIBLE.
The playbook was designed to make them champions and to play at their highest ELEVATION,
The Bible was designed for us to attain eternal life and SALVATION.
On the football field, the players play hard and sometimes get BLISTERS,
In the church, we play hard with our brothers and SISTERS.
On the football field, you want a wall that won't BUDGE,
In the game of life, you tear down the wall of sin because you are JUDGED.
On the playing field, both teams are pretty even and LEVEL,
On our field of play, we are up against the DEVIL.
It is important that every football player believes that they can WIN,
It is even more important that we believe so that we can conquer SIN.
In the football game, some of the players get down on one knee to execute the PLAY,

In the game of life, all of the believers get down on both knees to
Pray.
When they go up against their opponent, they are wearing a helmet
and shoulder pads that protect them very Nice,
When we go up against the devil, we have the armor of Christ.
In the game of football, it's important that everyone have faith to
win, down to the last Man.
In the game of life, you must have faith to get to heaven—the prom-
ised Land.
On Sundays, the players nourish their bodies with Gatorade,
On Sundays, we nourish ourselves with what God Made.
They are taught to block so that running backs can get Through,
We are taught that we should let His light shine Through.
The offensive line practices to make that perfect Hole,
We pray for our brother's Soul.
In the Super Bowl, the winner has a celebration in their Hometown,
In the game of life, if we endure, we will celebrate in heaven. How
does that Sound?
And like the Super Bowl, in the game of life, there is no overtime.
They call it sudden Death,
But this is how they differ when you take your last Breath.
In the Super Bowl, they have five quarters to separate the Tie.
In the game of life, when you die, you Die.
The Super Bowl is just an earthly game that we Play,
The game of life is a serious game where we all must Pay.
Please don't wait. Your life is almost Over,
Do you really want to be looking over your Shoulder?
So I ask you, are you ready? Are you ready for some Football?
Are you ready? Are you ready for Christ?
I am going to end this Story,
By giving God all the Glory.

Humility

When we open our eyes each and every DAY,
We must meditate on our Lord and Savior and PRAY.
And remember that when our Lord and Savior speak to Us,
Our hearts should be filled with compassion and TRUST.
We must be humble in the Lord's SIGHT,
To do His will and to do it RIGHT.
Humility is a virtue of its OWN,
It gives us love and compassion for family, friends, and HOME.
Humility is not a know-it-all ATTITUDE,
It is one of compassion, love, and GRATITUDE.
It's a combination of mind and heart that listens as God SPEAK,
It changes his personality and makes him loving and MEEK.
He hears what God has to say and understands all the TRUTH,
And by reading God's word, he has all the PROOF.
Being humble helps us search beyond ourselves for the answers to
    serious questions in LIFE,
Questions that cause heartache and questions that cause us STRIFE.
It helps us turn to the one and only source of truth—Jesus Christ,
    our Lord and SAVIOR,
It is because of Him that we change our human BEHAVIOR.
He helps us UNDERSTAND,
That He is both God and MAN.
He also helps us understand the mysteries of life, you SEE,
Those mysteries beyond the natural intellect of you and ME.
In closing, the grace of God is able to teach and form our humble
    SOUL,
And fill it with clarity of vision for the young and the OLD.

And accept God's truths that are embedded in our MIND,
And preach His doctrine and gospel time after TIME.
You have just heard a humble poem and STORY,
That was written for God's GLORY.

What Is Your Excuse?

What is your excuse? I have heard them ALL,
From every woman, every man, and every CHILD.
Why won't you try to earn salvation TODAY,
Let's open the Bible and see what God has to SAY.
Just because you are a member of a church, it may not give you all that you NEED,
Read Matthew 7:21, and please take HEED.
Not everyone who says to me, Lord, Lord, will enter the kingdom of HEAVEN,
But only he who does the will of my Father, who is in HEAVEN.
And the great question is, have I been born of GOD?
And am I showing by my life that I am a child of GOD (John 3:3)?
If you can answer yes to those two things that I have READ,
Then you will be one of God's children, and you will not remain DEAD.
Your next excuse is that maybe you think that I am good enough. Hey, I did my PART,
But God says you are a sinner. He knows your HEART (Romans 3:10, Romans 3:23, Luke 16:15, Proverbs 21:2).
Your next excuse might be that I am not good enough to be a Christian, you SEE,
But remember, Jesus came to save sinners like you and ME (Luke 19:10).
Next, you might think that you are too great a sinner to be saved by His GRACE,
And that the fruits of heaven you will never TASTE (Mark 2:17, Romans 5:8, Ephesians 2:8).

Another excuse you might make is that I am not ready now. I am
 going to WAIT,
Listen, this may be your last opportunity to determine your FATE
 (Luke 12:19–20).
Act now. What are you waiting FOR?
Without salvation, hell is in STORE.
You never know; Jesus may come today or TOMORROW (Matthew
 24:44, Matthew 25:13),
And your heart and soul will be filled with SORROW.
It will be too late THEN,
To enter the kingdom of HEAVEN (Jeremiah 8:20).
How would you feel on judgment DAY?
If your only excuse was that I wasn't ready TODAY.

Salt of the Earth

This is what it means to be the salt of the Earth,
To help others go to heaven and manage God's Turf.
You see, salt is a preservative. When added to food, it enhances the Taste,
Food is made to be enjoyed, not to Waste.
You see, salt, when used, disappears right before our Eyes,
Like our Lord and Savior when He enters our Lives.
You must understand that when our Lord goes In,
He preserves us from Sin.
He brings out the flavor of holiness that is evident to Others,
Everyone sees it—all my sisters and Brothers.
When others use salt, it brings out understanding and Clarity,
When it enters your soul, you do acts of Charity.
One of the greatest acts of charity is to forgive someone who has sinned against You,
But our Lord says that not only are we to reject the temptation to "get back," but we must pray for them Too.
And the reason that we must imitate the abundant mercy that God gives Us,
It is because it will transform us into being righteous and Just.
In a sense, the evil that another does to You,
Has the potential to be transformed into a gift that was given to You.
This is a very practical gift that God wants us to Embrace,
It transforms us and makes us holy by loving the human Race.
I am going to end this poem and Story,
By giving God all the Glory.

"Here He Is!"

Imagine this: You have just shot a 150-lb. Deer,
One that you have been chasing for over a Year.
You think that it was a white Tail,
So you climb down from the deer stand to follow the blood Trail.
You set off to follow, and your emotions are running High,
Anxious to follow the blood trail and see where he is going to Die.
After one hundred yards or So,
The blood trail gets thin, and you don't know which way to Go.
So back to the camp you go to get your buddies to help you Find,
That trail of blood that eludes you time after Time.
So we all spread out, looking for the blood Trail,
Anxious to find the body of that elusive white Tail.
Then someone shouted out, "Here he is!" We found the Deer,
This is what everyone wants to Hear.
The moral of this story is that, as followers of Jesus, we often need to stop where we are and make sure that we are still on the blood trail, you See,
A trail of blood that pertains to you and a trail of blood that pertains to Me.
After all, it was His blood that was shed so that we would be Forgiven,
And have a chance to be with Him in Heaven.
So when you seem to be veering off the blood trail of our Lord and Savior,
Make sure you have someone you can call to get you back on track with your human Behavior.
And always remember those three famous words, "Here he is!" and that is what you want to Say,

Because it is the blood of Jesus that keeps the devil Away.
I am going to end this poem and Story,
By giving God all the Glory.

Is It about Me? Is It about You?

It's about me, and it's not about me
It's about you, and it's not about you
It's about the body of Christ, you see
The body of Christ that is in you
The body of Christ that is in me
It's hard to explain the feeling that we get
But it is also a feeling that we will never ever Forget
We once had a heart that was on the ground
Like a rock, hard and embedded
But now we have a heart that is soft
And one that is shredded
With a change of heart comes a change of mind as well
A change that everyone can easily tell
As we sit here on Sunday and Wednesday night
There is a transformation in the people sitting on
Our left and one sitting on our right
It is the presence of God touching our heart
With a feeling that will never ever depart
It's the word of God going through our ears
Into our hearts, minds, and souls and bring us to tears
And when you hear a song that you think pertains to you
It brings you to your knees, the way God wanted it to
What gets me is people going to another church
Sitting there in a pew, like a bird on a perch
Sitting there and learning nothing about God
But every now and then, giving their heads a little nod
I know because I used to sit there time and time again
Waiting for the services to begin

We are so fortunate to be here today to hear what God has to say
Today we are going to discuss what other churches say and do
So that you don't go over there and sit in their pew
These things that we are about to talk about, please take heed
And whatever you do, do not give them Godspeed
And when you leave here and go out into the world
And people try to change your mind
Don't believe them every single time
They may be innocent people who don't know the truth
Open your Bible and show them the proof
God made this Bible for a reason
To teach people, season after season

His Way

I want to wake up today with one thing in MIND,
To do the will of God rather than the will of MINE.
To do them out of love rather than FEAR,
To do them, for He has been so DEAR.

You see, deep down inside, He wants us to live in this world in such a WAY,
That we touch someone's heart each and every DAY.
Because we are made in the image of God, our Lord and SAVIOR,
We must take control of our human BEHAVIOR.
And to do His will at all COST,
For He came for the sinners. He came for the LOST.

Then there is our heavenly Father; if the truth be TOLD,
He is in full CONTROL.
When I wrote this, the pandemic had been going on for approximately ten months to DATE,
And He is the only one who can determine our FATE.

And remember, in Louisiana, we were on our third STORM,
Come on, guys, that's out of the NORM.
Are you kidding me? In Lake Charles, in less than a month, we got hit with two category THREES,
Bringing the people of Lake Charles to their KNEES.

Then all those fires in California and riots all over our great LAND,
Could all of this be part of God's PLAN.

Not to mention those who have not worked in seven to eight months
     or So,
So broke that they don't know which way to Go.
Don't you UNDERSTAND?
He wants you humbled and broken with a contrite heart, down to
     the very last MAN.
He wants you to surrender to Him, heart, body, and SOUL,
He wants to save the young as well as the OLD.

I know that some of you don't get it, but that's OKAY,
I promise you, this will not keep God AWAY.
He will not forsake you, and I tell you WHY,
Because God said it in the Bible, and God cannot LIE.

He is working on you as we SPEAK,
Not just today, but week after WEEK.
He will never forsake you. He is there for the long HAUL,
He was there for the apostles. He was there for PAUL.
So let's start things a little differently TODAY,
By getting out of bed and doing things His WAY.
And remember, all these things that I said are TRUE,

So now I ask you, WHAT ARE YOU GOING TO DO?

Pride vs. Humility

Pride says, "I need this. I want this. I deserve this."
Humility says, "He needs this. They want this. You deserve eternal bliss."
Pride says, "God, I am so much better than that other guy."
Humility says, "Lord, have mercy on me. I will be a sinner until I die."
Pride criticizes others to tear them down.
Humility praises others to build them up and make them heaven-bound.
Pride says, "Don't tell me anything. I know the way."
Humility says, "Thanks for your advice and help. You made my day."
Pride says, "I can do all things. Look at me."
Humility says, "I can do all things through Christ, who strengthens me."
Pride exalts himself. But God will resist that man.
Humility humbles himself before God, and God will lift that man.
Pride says, "Look at what I did. Look at me."
Humility says, "See what God has done in me."

The difference between pride and humility is like comparing the difference between light and darkness. When "the light" came into this world, the perfect example of humility was revealed to us.

Prayer

We all struggle with PRAYER,
We would not admit it. We wouldn't DARE.
Prayer is active, not passive, and it starts in our minds, then down to our HEART (Proverbs 4:23),
Then out of our mouths, comes our very THOUGHT.
A prayer that takes just seconds to SAY,
But one that may change our paths or our WAY.
A prayer that will change our lives for the BEST,
A prayer that will make us different from the REST.
When each and every prayer crosses our lips, it plays a ROLE,
Touching our hearts, touching our SOUL.
Prayer must come from the heart—from WITHIN,
When we pray, we must be pure of SIN (John 9:31).
For sin will keep us from God's open ARMS (Isaiah 59:2, Psalms 66:13),
For He knows of sins deceiving CHARMS (Proverbs 31:30, 2 Corinthians 11:3).
Always pray to God, you SEE (Matthew 6:6, James 1:5),
For Jesus is the mediator for you and ME (1 Timothy 2:5).
He is the mediator for the LOST,
He fulfilled that role when He died on the CROSS (Matthew 27:32–56).
Sometimes, we might tell someone, I will pray for YOU,
But do we remember, or do we forget that TOO?
When we don't pray for that person, is it a LIE?
And will we be judged on that when we DIE?
So when you offer to pray for someone in NEED,

Remember, you might be judged for doing that DEED.
I would like to end this STORY,
By giving God all the GLORY.

Power

Every time I read the Bible, there is something that I Feel,
Something that is hard to explain, but something that is very Real.
And when you read the scriptures and feel the power and Glory,
You sense that this book is not just another Story.
I am here to tell you that this book is Alive,
Listen to it if you want to eternally Survive.
God wrote this book in such a Way,
That if you read it, you would adhere to what He had to Say.
So when you read the scripture, read it like a Prayer,
Very slowly and with a lot of Care.
For these scriptures are about your Life,
Some filled with joy; some filled with Strife.
There is power in every Verse,
The more you read, the more you hunger and Thirst.
For there is one thing I want you to Understand,
That God wants no one to perish, down to the very last Man.
In order to be saved, you must listen to what God has to Say,
Please don't go on your own, and let's do it His Way.
I would like to end this Story,
By giving God all the Glory.

An Element of Prayer

Matthew 6:6–8
But when you pray, go into your room and close the Door,
And pray to your Father, who never keeps Score.
Your Father, who is Unseen,
Your Father, who wants you on His Team.
Then your Father, who sees what is done in Secret,
Will reward you, and you do not have to repeat It.
For He will answer your prayers with His divine will from up Above,
For He is a God of care—a God of Love.
God isn't interested in big, large words that you Know,
He is interested in the feeling of the heart that you have to Show.
And remember, you cannot put your heavenly Father to Task,
He knows what you are going to say way before you Ask.

When Do We Keep Our Mouth Shut? Don't Open Your Mouth

1. If you are mad at someone, think before you speak, because if the truth is told, anger can cause you to lose control (Proverbs 14:17).
2. Never make a poor decision based on information that you might lack. Don't decide before you have all of the facts (Proverbs 18:13).
3. Don't open your mouth before you have verified the story. The person you just put in shame might be the one of glory (Deuteronomy 17:6).
4. Watch what you say to one another. You might offend a weaker brother.
5. Don't open your mouth if it's a poor reflection of your human behavior.
6. When you get tempted to joke about sin, always remember Adam and what sin did to him (Proverbs 14:9).
7. Don't open your mouth. You might be ashamed of what you just said because you will be the only one lying in that bed (Proverbs 8:8).

Now, What?

There's more to
Milk
and
Honey

Poems from Lou Palmisano
A Stage 4 Cancer Survivor

There's More

Read this slowly, and please ponder every line to know that our heavenly Father created all these things because He is so divine.

Let's go back a couple of thousand years. They have a man and a woman in the desert, and this guy walked up to them and said, "Can we talk? I have a lot to tell you."

This guy named Joey said, "Sure, go ahead."

With that, the man picked up a handful of sand, sifted through it, and left one grain of sand in the middle of his hand. He then said, "This sand represents the size of earth in outer space, and earth is kind of round in shape, like a ball floating by itself. The closest planet to us is Venus, which is thirty-eight million kilometers away."

Joey and the woman just stared at him, like a deer in headlights. Joey said, "Wow!"

The guy said, "Sit back and relax. There's more. Do you see the sun up there? It is ninety-three million miles away from the earth, and it is in constant orbit around the sun. Now the earth is tilted 23.5 degrees, so as it goes around the sun, the earth is tilted toward the sun in the summer. As it continues in orbit, it is tilted away from the sun in the winter. That is why we have the four seasons: summer, fall, winter, and spring. Now listen closely. As the earth goes in orbit around the sun, the moon is in orbit around the earth. What we have here is an orbit inside another orbit."

Joey said, "You mean, as the earth is going around the sun, the moon is going around the earth."

The guy said, "That's right, and are you ready for this? Both the moon and the earth are traveling toward and around the sun at sixty-five thousand miles per hour. And at the same time, the earth is spinning one thousand miles per hour on its axis. But listen, Joey, there's more. The earth's atmosphere protects us from a couple of things. First, it protects us from meteors and meteorites coming from outer space. They simply burn up before they hit the earth. Next, the atmosphere protects us from the super cold weather in outer space."

"How cold is it in outer space?" Joey asked.

The man said, "Minus 459 degrees, and if we were one degree away from the sun, we would freeze, or one degree closer to the sun, we would burn up. Speaking of exact, the earth must contain the right amount of oxygen. Too much, and when you light a fire, it will explode. Too little, and you could not light a fire or breathe. By the way, Joey, by volume, dry air contains 78.09% nitrogen, 20.95% oxygen, 0.93% argon, and 0.0397% carbon dioxide."

Joey asked, "Where does oxygen come from?"

The man said, "I am happy you asked that question, Joey. You see, 20% comes from the grass and trees, and 80% comes from the ocean. That's why fish can live underwater. Speaking of water, Joey, the earth has a system for purifying ocean water. You see, ocean water evaporates and causes rain clouds. The salt content in the water burns off and pours waterfalls to the earth as rain."

Joey said, "I get it. The water that we drink is recycled over and over again."

"Correct! By the way, Joey, I forgot to tell you that all the stars that you see at night are actually suns. The largest sun is so big that if you were in a plane and traveling at nine hundred kilometers per hour, it would take 1,100 years to go around it one time."

Joey said, "Are you kidding me?"

"No," the man said, "that's a fact. But wait, there's more. Let's go back to what we were talking about—water. Imagine the water that we drink. It is colorless, odorless, tasteless, and contains no calories, carbohydrates, proteins, or anything else that has merit, yet it is essential for life. But there's more. Water freezes from top to bottom, so fish can live. Water is a universal solvent where minerals and pills can be carried through the body for nourishment. But wait, Joey, there's more. Everything needs water—plants, animals, and especially fish. Speaking of plants, a seed must die before it grows again."

Joey said, "I don't understand that."

The man said, "That's another story. Well, Joey, how are you doing?"

Joey said, "It's hard to comprehend all of this."

"But wait, there's more. Let's go back to fish for a minute. Some fish multiply by spawning. The female lays her eggs somewhere in the water, and the male comes along and somehow finds them and fertilizes the eggs, and fish life is created."

"Wow! That is something else," Joey said.

The man said, "Hang on, Joey, there's more. Since we were talking about fish reproducing, they have this fish called the angler-fish. It lives at the bottom of the ocean. It has a pole-like member coming out of its head with a light at the end of it. The light attracts other fish, and they eat the other fish. Now the female is about three feet long, and the male fish is about three inches long."

Joey said, "How do they reproduce? I bet that it is something weird."

"Well, Joey, as the female fish, which is three feet long, is swimming, the male fish, which is three inches long, bites her along the flank. As he sinks his teeth into her skin, the fluids from her body enter his mouth, and his body dissolves inside her body. The only thing left are his gonads on her flank. When the female wants to have babies, she uses them. Well, Joey, what do you think about that?"

"I think I am happy that I am not a fish."

"But wait, Joey, there's more. I have another fish story for you. Now the stingray has between five and ten babies at a time. How come the babies, which are inside the mother's stomach, don't hurt her with those barbs at the end of their tails?"

Joey said, "I have no idea."

Well, Joey, you see, when the babies are inside the mother's stomach, the barbs are covered with a heavy or thick skin. When it hits oxygen when they are born, the covering dissolves."

Joey said, "All of this does not seem possible."

"But wait, Joey, there's more. How many baby crabs can a blue claw crab have at a time?"

Joey said, "I am guessing about fifty to sixty, maybe."

"No, Joey, depending on the size of the crab, between half a million and eight million at one time. You see, Joey, crabs are in the food chain."

"Wow!" Joey said.

"But wait, Joey, there's more. Next, Joey, I want to tell you about the chicken. How long do you think it takes a chicken to hatch from when the egg was first laid?"

"Well," Joey said, "the chicken and the chick to scale are about the same size as a baby and its mother. It has a heart, eyes, legs, veins, and feet, and, I am sure, some small brain, maybe six months."

"No, Joey, just twenty-one days."

Joey said, "How is that possible?"

"I don't really know, Joey. I guess partly because it may be in the food chain again. Remember, Joey, a mother takes nine months to have her baby, and God wants that mother to carry her baby for nine months so that she can grow to love that baby when he or she is born. As opposed to the chicken that can't grow to love her chick in just twenty-one days. But wait, Joey, there's more. The birth of a baby is amazing. Two liquids come together, and a baby is born with everything. We are talking about bones, ribs, two lungs, and two kidneys. That's right, a spare lung and a spare kidney, a liver, miles of veins, two eyes to see, two ears to hear, a tongue to talk, a mouth to eat, hands to hold things, feet to walk, an elbow on the arm to eat, a knee on the leg to walk, and a brain that controls the whole body. All from two fluids coming together. Now get this: six weeks after conception, a heartbeat appears. From where?"

Joey and the woman shook their heads in amazement.

The man said, "But wait, Joey, there's more. In time, there will be seven billion people walking here on earth. All of them will have different fingerprints and different DNA. And, Joey, I will tell you later what DNA means. But right now, I want you two to rap your heads around this: when God made man, He formed Him from the dust of the earth and then blew into his nostrils a living being, and thus a man was made. And then He took one of Adam's ribs and made his wife Eve."

Joey said, "Why are you telling us all of this now?"

"Well, Joey, you see, the world that we are living in is very complicated and, in the future, will be full of distractions."

"Like what?" Joey asked.

"Well, Joey, man is going to work more hours, and his wife might have to work. Then there are kids, sex, alcohol, drugs, television, then the computer, then peer pressure, a lack of government leadership, and a lack of unity with the churches. You see, Joey, there are so many distractions that man cannot stay focused on God. So I wanted to show you the power of God and what He has made so that we can make time for the one true God. That includes God the Father, God the Son, and God the Holy Spirit."

Joey said, "Wait, hold on. That's three Gods. You said one God. What's up? I counted three."

"Okay, Joey. I know it's confusing, but listen. We live in a three-dimensional world, and time is the fourth dimension. God lives in the sixth, seventh—who knows dimension. In our world, $1 + 1 + 1 = 3$. In God's world, $1 \times 1 \times 1 = 1$. God can be everywhere at the same time. Picture God as one being with certain characteristics or personalities. Like the huge sun as the Father, the light that it gives off as the Son, and the warmth that it gives off as the Holy Spirit."

Joey said, "That kind of makes sense."

"Good, Joey, but there's more. Because of the sins of man, God sent His Son Jesus to earth, born of a virgin."

Joey said, "Hold on, virgin birth?"

"That's right. God can do anything, as I have been telling you. Trust me, Joey, you must have faith."

"You guessed it," Joey said. "What is faith? Faith is the substance of things hoped for and the evidence of things not seen. Because without faith, you cannot please God, and you cannot make it to heaven."

"I know, Joey, just listen. There's more. Heaven is a place where there will be no more tears and no more pain. Hopefully, we will be in the presence of God, where there will be an abundance of love and an abundance of light. You certainly don't want to go to hell. Hell is a place where the worm will never die. A place of torment filled with intense heat, darkness, and despair. That's why God sent His Son

Jesus, who will die on the cross, for the forgiveness of our sins. And who, after three days, will rise from the dead, and He will come again to judge the living and the dead."

Joey said, "This sounds very serious."

"It is, Joey. We are talking about eternity."

Joey said, "How do you get this faith?"

The man said, "By hearing and reading the word of God—that is the Bible. You see, Joey, Jesus Christ will be the light of the world, and when you read the Bible and do what the Bible commands, it will change you into the image and likeness of Him, and then you will live in heaven for eternity. But listen, Joey, there's more. In the years to come, they will celebrate the birth of Jesus every year. They will call the celebration Christmas. The word Christ is in the first six letters. Let's keep Christ first in our Christmas and first in our lives."

"Wow! This blows my mind," Joey said.

"But wait, Joey, there's more. One day, someone might use your name as the elf on a shelf. The elf on the shelf is used by parents to make their children listen at Christmas time."

Joey started laughing. "My dad didn't use an elf on the shelf. He used a belt on the shelf."

For the first time, the woman raised her hand and said, "Sir, can I ask you a question?"

"Sure, go ahead."

"What might my name be used for?"

"What is your name?" the man asked.

"My name is Mary."

"Well, Mary, I have been looking for you for a long time. My name is Gabe, short for Gabriel, and your boyfriend's name is Joey, short for Joseph. Come, let's have a seat. There's more, a lot more, that I must tell you."

What the Cross Means to Me

Let's imagine tonight that we all took the place of Jesus, if that's all right.
Stephanie, can you imagine if you took Jesus's place on trial?
Would you object, or would you be in denial?
Diane, can you imagine how you would have felt that day?
If they had arrested you and taken you away,
Can you imagine how you would have felt, Tim?
If you would have heard those words, Crucify him!
Margie, how would you feel being scourged and whipped time and time again?
Your skin is being torn apart, thinking, *Is this ever going to end?*
Amy, how about the thorns that they shoved into your head?
The pain was so intense that you wished you were dead.
Bob, what could you say,
As they asked you to carry the cross all the way?
Barbara, can you imagine what you would have done,
As they drove the nails into your hands one by one?
David, as they nailed your feet to the cross,
Would you begin saying, "Forgive them, Father, for they are lost"?
Ann, can you imagine you hanging there on the cross,
Looking down at your crying mother on her knees?
And asking the apostle that you love to watch over her if you please.
Ken, can you imagine what you would think,
If they offered you what was on that sponge to drink?
Beverly, imagine how you would have felt, hanging there in all your pain and agony and praying to your Father.
And someone plunges a sword in your side, and out comes blood and water.

Marcia, how would you feel if you were His mother, Mary?
Looking up at her Son, He gave you a helpless smile and a loving
　　nod.
And you, not believing that they just crucified the Son of God.

If each of these things had happened to one of us, that would be hard
　　to believe.
But all these things happened to one man; we can even begin to
　　conceive.

Jesus was beaten and scourged on His knees and hands,
Because Pilate caved in to the people's demands.
The fact that they tortured our Lord and Savior,
Because of their own human behavior.
We must remember that Jesus was only thirty-three years old when
　　he took His last breath,
And He was the only one to ever conquer death.
Jesus was the final sacrifice for all,
The old, the young, the short, the weak, and the tall—two thousand
　　years have come and gone at a furious pace.
And today, he is the central figure of the entire human race,
His birth (BC) and death (AD) have been measurements of time that
　　are still used today.
Not too bad for a man without a country, wouldn't you say?

This is what the cross means to me,
Because of His death, we were set free.
What a wonderful position God has put us in!
We no longer have to be slaves to sin.
It's like waking up to a new life at the crack of dawn,
Isn't it wonderful that we had a chance to be reborn?

About the Author

The author of this book has had several life-changing experiences. An example came about one day at work, as one of his coworkers was leaving town to take another job. When asked where he was going, he said, "To the land of milk and honey." He was asked where that was. The coworker said that it was California. For years, the author thought that the land of milk and honey was really California.

One day, while he was in church with his mother, the minister said, "The land of milk and honey is the promised land that is in the Bible." When the minister finished that statement, he held the Bible high over his head and said, "And this is the word of GOD." The author thought, *Here, this man has the word of God, and I don't!* He bought a Bible and has been on fire ever since! But wait, his story doesn't stop here!

In 2019, he was diagnosed with stage 4 kidney cancer. It had spread to his lungs, vena cava, and arm. He was told that he had less than a year to live. It was in the hospital that he had an encounter with an angelic being (Hebrew 1:14, Psalm 91:11). They were bronze in color (Ezekiel 1:7, Revelation 1:15). The author thought to himself that he now knows how an innocent man who has been put in jail feels. When he told his story about seeing angels, no one believed him. He also had numerous dreams that all came true. Oh, and by the way, there is no active cancer in his body. It is in remission.

The poems that you will read are thought-provoking, and here is a final thought: Are you spending more time planning a vacation than planning for your eternal salvation?

Printed in the USA
CPSIA information can be obtained
at www.ICGtesting.com
LVHW040607190924
791303LV00003B/413

9 798891 308213